IF CARS COULD TALK

ESSAYS ON URBANISM

IF

ESSAYS

CARS

ON

COULD

URBANISM

TALK

William H. Fain, Jr.

First Edition

Published in the United States of America in 2012 by Balcony Press.

No part of this book may be reproduced in any manner without written permission
except in the case of brief quotations embodied in critical articles and reviews.

For information contact Balcony Media, Inc., 512 E. Wilson Avenue, Suite 213,
Glendale California 91206. www.balconypress.com

Design by Sarah Carr, www.heredesign.co.uk
Printing and production by Navigator Cross-media
Printed in South Korea

If Cars Could Talk © 2012 William H. Fain Jr.

Library of Congress Control Number: 2011961118
ISBN 978-1-890449-58-2

For Jennifer, Elizabeth & Margaret

CONTENTS

FOREWORD

The first thing you should know about Bill Fain is that he is an urban designer. He's an architect too, but his main interest is urban design. Urban design is a way of thinking about the world we build. It includes both architecture and city planning, but it goes beyond both. Fain thinks about buildings, but he's more concerned with the outdoor spaces that buildings shape, the streets and squares and parks and other places, good and bad, that make up the public world in which we spend much of our lives. He cares about poverty and politics, too, about public transit and smoggy freeways, about schools and riverfronts and much else. He's especially concerned about the invasion of the automobile into American life in the twentieth century and the ways in which it has undermined civic and community life.

Most books of this kind are written by professional writers or academics. Fain is neither, although he's done a good deal of teaching. He's a practitioner. He practices what he preaches. The lessons he draws come from his own experience, enriched by his wide reading. The book can be thought of as a sequence of ten sermons delivered to students by a guy who spends most of his time out in the world working in the complexity of real situations.

I've known Bill Fain since he was a city planner in Boston in the 1970s, but I was still astonished, reading this book, at the range of his activity For more than twenty years he's been the partner in charge of urban design for a major firm in Los Angeles, with work all over the world. In the early 1970s he served in the fabled Urban Design Group under Mayor Lindsay in Manhattan. Later he worked on housing for HUD in Washington. Recent clients have included American Indians in Oklahoma and international corporations in China. When he was a Fellow at the American Academy in Rome, he investigated the relation of the Tiber River to its urban and rural context. On another grant he studied the urbanism of Paris and London. As an urban designer should be, Bill is interested in more or less everything, because more or less everything is involved in making a city.

Of course, Bill doesn't merely practice. He also looks and reads. He cites authors as diverse as Richard Sennett, Rousseau, Gandhi, Lao Tzu, Michael Sorkin, William Wordsworth, among others. To illustrate points, he reproduces images from such painters as Wayne Thiebaud, Ed Ruscha, Ron Davis, David Hockney and Chris Burden. You'd never know it from this book, but Bill is a talented artist himself. He returned from Rome with a masterful booklet of casual sketches of Italy.

Bill is seldom afraid to state an opinion. He hates the view, popularized not long ago by the architect Rem Koolhaus, that the true purpose of cities today is shopping and consumption. He agrees with the great urbanist Jane Jacobs that designers and planners should not be in the business of shaping the world to fit their own beliefs, but should rather find ways to help the rest of us achieve the life we want and need. He thinks most buildings shouldn't be solo performers. Instead, he suggests that a building should be in some way incomplete, so that only as it gathers with other buildings to shape a public place does it begin to participate in something complete.

No one knows more than Bill Fain about the problems that beset the world's cities. But Fain welcomes every problem as a learning experience. His optimism illuminates this book. He's convinced that with enough common sense and fellow-feeling, we'll do better.

Robert Campbell
Architecture Critic, *Boston Globe*

PREFACE

I love cities. I made a decision in the late 1960s to work on them. Although this collection of essays often refers to conditions in Los Angeles, my perspective is informed by experience with urban design in other locations, both international and domestic. I believe there is a little of Los Angeles in every modern city, be it Boston, New York, San Francisco, Beijing, London or Paris. Lessons learned here apply everywhere.

I have been fortunate enough to live in a number of world cities, mostly as a result of fellowships. In 2002, I completed a term at the American Academy in Rome as a Rolland Fellow. During my tenure, I had the opportunity to study and design the reconnection of the Tiber River to the everyday life of Rome. In the 1970s, I was fortunate to receive another two fellowships from the National Endowment for the Humanities and the National Endowment for the Arts, both of which focused on urban design. The Humanities fellowship enabled a year of studying the planning and design of London and Paris.

If Cars Could Talk draws upon all of these experiences.

Cities have been designed and redesigned for the car, bringing into focus issues of scale, separation, environmental quality and the consumption of economic and natural resources. In the competition for scarce tax dollars, the car is given more importance than public transit, open space, libraries, schools and other cultural services essential to a civilized society. As these car-enabling environments continually affect our society's values, we become part of a vicious circle.

The car is king in Los Angeles. It is ironic to design for humans when so much of our environment is planned to accommodate the car. Our high regard for cars and the personal mobility they provide has become an extension of what we view as our "personal freedom." Our identities and status are wrapped up in our cars. In L.A. it is often said that "you are what you drive." Although I was aware of the hyper-valuation of cars in the Los Angeles landscape, I hadn't realized the complexity of this relationship until I returned in 1980 and worked on an early plan for Universal Studios in Hollywood. Knowing I spent ten years working on the East Coast, Al Dorskind, MCA-Universal's senior vice president of real estate, told me, "…when we do architecture and planning in Los Angeles we start with the car and, in particular, parking." Much of a project's budget is spent for parking; road capacities at rush hours determine the amount of density entitled for a given site.

As other world cities are redeveloped and restructured as economic engines, the importance we give these other priorities will determine how successful we are in maintaining our edge in an increasingly competitive global economy. I do not believe that people will stop using cars nor do I believe this is even desirable. However, the future of the city cannot tolerate the cost of a "car-centric" infrastructure.

In the early 1970s I worked in New York Mayor John Lindsay's Urban Design Group at the Office of Midtown Planning and Development. He had assembled a group of young, creative and highly motivated architects under the leadership of Jaquelin Robertson, Richard Weinstein, Myles Weintraub and Jonathan Barnett. We worked on strategic assignments for an array of public projects and, very importantly, special purpose districts. These districts were "as-of-right" frameworks for guiding development decisions for specific locations, particularly in Manhattan, and included Fifth Avenue, the Theater District along Broadway, the Madison Avenue Mall and the Greenwich Street District in Lower Manhattan. They had many design provisions intended to address the specific needs of their respective neighborhoods. For example, the Fifth Avenue District was intended to stabilize retail on the avenue by limiting the number of banks and airline offices which are low pedestrian generating uses. Their rents were subsidized through advertising budgets because of the prestige of the Fifth Avenue address. Because they were willing to pay exorbitant rents, these uses were pushing out viable retail. At the same time, the district provided incentives for new development to re-establish residential land use.

The Fifth Avenue Special Purpose District was the first mixed-use zoning district in the United States.[01] Unlike earlier developments such as Battery Park City, these districts were structured to allow individual property owners to develop according to the zoning provisions and market conditions, and were not dependent upon public land assemblage. A number of years later, during work with the Boston Redevelopment Agency, I encountered a different approach that was more project-focused, favoring the creation of "transformational projects" like the Prudential Center in Back Bay, the Downtown Park Plaza and the New England Merchant Bank. Developments such as these were targeted to generate market share by concentrating resources on specific sites. Land policy in Boston was, and continues to be, determined by deal making instead of as-of-right zoning. What worked in New York did not necessarily work in Boston for a variety of reasons, such as geography (i.e., various road systems), real estate market dynamics, city culture and community participation.

Understanding the workings of real estate is fundamental to successful urban design. After graduate school, I worked for a public-private development company, the New Communities Development Corporation at the Department of Housing and Urban Development (HUD) in Washington D.C. I was one of several professionals hired to help work out financially troubled "new towns", which were located principally in the middle and eastern United States. Several colleagues from Harvard were also hired, and the team worked under an inspiring young Justice Department lawyer named James Dausch, who was brought to New Communities by Carla Hills, then secretary of HUD under President Ford. It was a compelling assignment for me. I was able to work on re-scoping the new town development programs and their implementation plans with revised assumptions about market absorption and phased infrastructure costs. In many cases traditional market studies were not available and our team had to improvise by using local homebuilder data regarding housing starts and building permit activity. Reports were given regularly to Dausch, who was able to make strategic decisions about land take downs and grants for infrastructure and public services.

By the election in 1976, Dausch was interested in using a similar methodology to assess inner city projects that could help transform downtowns and inner city neighborhoods across the country. Dausch was from Baltimore, and having witnessed the transformation of Baltimore's Charles Center and Inner Harbor, saw the potential of making similar efforts elsewhere. He chose me to lead a team to assess potential federal assistance for projects sponsored by local governments. We visited and analyzed over twenty cities and made recommendations to HUD senior management about ways to scope and finance the projects. This study provided the foundation for the first Enterprise Zone program of the late 1970s.

During one of my trips to the West Coast in 1978, I met William L. Pereira, the iconic and prolific Southern California architect. Pereira was very interested in the "big picture" and had a notable history of designing large, challenging projects. We discussed many of these during our meeting, which lasted nearly six hours. Pereira was a broad thinker with a vivid imagination and a deep appreciation of culture and differing city forms. We found much common ground. Much of my work had been strategic and framework-driven. He completely understood what I was talking about. His work was driven by the same things for both public and private clients. Two years later I returned to Los Angeles to join Pereira's team and never left. My business partner, Scott Johnson, joined us in 1983, and in 1989, four years after Pereira's death, Scott and I transitioned the firm to Johnson Fain, Inc.

INTRODUCTION

02
Frameworks tend to be comprised of standards and guidelines applied "as-of-right" to a defined urban area. Standards are development requirements, while guidelines are elective provisions. Strategies pertain to redevelopment areas and tend to be less definitive, allowing for some degree of deal making between public officials and private developers. Projects are specific built properties, funded privately, publicly or through public-private joint ventures.

The essays of *If Cars Could Talk* are not meant to personify the car, but rather to focus on the humans who drive them. But one might suspect if a car could talk it would ask: "Why do you make such a fuss over me? Why do people spend so much of their resources on me? Why do architects and city planners give such high priority to me in their designs for neighborhoods and downtowns?"

The evolution of the city is based on a multitude of decisions on many levels. Enabling or responding to the realities of an evolutionary process should be a primary consideration in any urban design assignment. Understanding and respecting that others are the decision-makers leads to planning that engenders a sense of neighborhood pride and identity—and ultimately contributes to the prosperity of the city. Each situation is unique, as no two urban contexts are identical. There is little opportunity to model a generic solution able to address multiple settings. Therefore understanding a city's setting—its history, politics, economics, demographics, culture and ecological landscape—is central to the urban design task. Starting with these understandings, urban design concepts evolve from listening, interpreting and guiding decisions for areas of the city so that both private and civic purposes are achievable.

Over the years, I have collaborated with both public and private clients, and my work—depending upon the assignment—has been strategic, framework and project-driven.[02] My public agency experience on the East Coast led me to believe that even private projects should have some public benefit, that it is better business to advance a project that includes a generous civic purpose. This has proven especially true in securing entitlements for large urban developments.

The essays in this volume span subjects relating to urbanism, architecture and urban design practices that have arisen during my career. Several of the essays address aspects of our society and culture, such as car use, that directly or indirectly affect the way urban design is practiced in the United States and abroad; others present artistic, spatial and compositional thoughts about designing urban-scale projects. The impetus for this collection originated from a lecture I gave at the Southern California Institute of Architecture (SCI-Arc) in early 2006, for which I created a list of the main principles that inform my approach to urban design:

1—URBAN DESIGN AND PUBLIC POLICY

Create public policy frameworks to bring certainty to development decision-making. Such frameworks are anticipatory, allowing for incremental change while providing flexibility according to market conditions. Examples of frameworks include specific plans and special purpose districts.

2—SYSTEMS FOR COLLECTIVE BENEFIT

Establish urban design frameworks that ensure collective benefits, including the environment and respect for nature,[03] providing an essential bridge between private gain and public benefit. Such frameworks can prevent projects from internalizing development benefits at the expense of the community, city and environment.

3—DEFERENCE TO OTHERS

Establish frameworks that allow others to act. Instead of viewing *pluralism* as mega-buildings with a variety of expressions, pluralism should be seen as an inclusive decision-making and development process, wherein many individuals are enabled to act. By means of deferential frameworks, urban designers can design cities without designing buildings.[04] The success of an urban design plan should be measured by how well others can act.

4—SPACE AS THE "OBJECT"

Reverse our obsession with building form, so that urban space is the predominant form to be measured, analyzed and designed, with

[03] Designing *with* nature is fundamental to designing sustainable environments. It is foremost in how architects design for the future. Ian McHarg's book *Design with Nature* and the plan and design for Sea Ranch by Larry Halprin, Charles Moore, Bill Turnbull, Donlyn Lyndon and Dick Whittaker are especially inspiring examples of this type of thinking and practice.

[04] As expressed by Jonathan Barnett in his 1974 book *Urban Design as Public Policy: Practical Methods for Improving Cities* (New York: Architectural Records Books, 1974).

05
The Grove and L.A. Live received public support based in part on creating "public space." However, what resulted were spaces described as "public" and yet deeply embedded within a private development, as happens all too often in Los Angeles. My belief is that a public plaza needs to have at least two sides fronting public roads, and preferably all four sides.

buildings evaluated on how well they create and support urban spaces and their activities. [05]

5—TIME-FORM

Treat urban environments as figure-ground fields that incrementally form and re-form over time based on the movement of people, capital, infrastructure and resources.

6—PAST AND FUTURE

Urban design solutions should draw upon what came before but also anticipate the future. Projects are placed in a continuum somewhere between being and becoming. Testing future scenarios, phasing and flexibility become important elements of project design.

7—STEPPING INTO A FLUID CONTEXT

Understand the implications and influence of building projects within their contexts. Context is not a static setting for a project, but rather a dynamic situation reflecting ever-changing social and economic conditions: local, regional and global. As such, an urban design intervention influences the situation it enters, becoming a context-maker as well as a context-responder.

8—BALANCING THE BIG AND THE SMALL

Good urban design balances a city's need for both big ideas and opportunities for countless small actions. For example, New York has benefitted from the work of Robert Moses and the advocacy of Jane Jacobs in becoming a great city.

9—NOT FORMULAIC

Good urban design offers creative conflict resolution, a process leading to customized solutions that cater to specific local needs. For public agencies, local market conditions determine methods for implementation, which require different types and degrees of public intervention. This determines the appropriate urban design framework for a local site.

10—TIMELESS SYSTEMS

Urban designers should study and employ systems that are simple and direct, universal and timeless, flexible and open-ended, an example of which is the age-old street grid.

These essays may overlap in places. The book is not intended to read as a continuum. Each essay focuses on a particular moment and subject. However, they each speak to the potential of the city and the emphasis we must give it to move urbanism forward.[06]

[06] Six of the essays were first published as the bi-monthly column "AIA Report," in *L.A. Architect*, today known as *Form* magazine. These were expanded and four others were added over the past year.

GOOD LIFE CITY

"The Good Life" reflects a universal desire, regardless of culture and history. This proved itself several years ago when our firm was invited to compete for the design of four square miles of Central Shanghai, a site located down the Huang Pu River across from the Pudong District. The site was an old naval air station, and like military closures in the U.S., China was decommissioning the base for conversion to civilian use. It was a sixteen-week competition between four firms with interim and final presentations. We were the only American team.

From the outset, we realized that the Chinese government had provided an open-ended program with unlimited possibilities. We found it impossible to present only one scheme, as was expected at the interim presentation. In order to flesh out the program, we developed three concepts involving substantially more work, but still a risk we had to take. Looking toward China's future and the expectations of the Chinese people, each option presented a "big idea." It was our hope that the reviewers would understand what we were presenting and select one concept for further development.

To an audience of 400 engineers and government officials, we first presented the "Green City" concept. This scheme represented an ecologically sustainable plan that resonated with efforts of the government to promote environmentally sensitive development. Next, we presented the "Knowledge City" concept. Understanding that China's future prosperity depends upon unleashing its intelligence through education, this plan augmented three surrounding universities with a central high-technology campus and satellite learning centers in the neighborhoods. The third option assumed a prosperous future for China, with its people having leisure time to enjoy the fruits of their labor. We termed this concept the "Good Life City," in which people live active outdoor lives, enjoying boating, golfing and tennis in a garden setting. Informality is this city's contour.

The audience seemed confounded by being offered more than one scheme. We were not certain that they were willing to play the conceptual game. The chief administrator understood what we were presenting, but we had no idea if she valued it. Following the presentation, teams returned to their home offices and waited for the government's comments. There were six weeks before the final presentation in Shanghai. The first and second weeks passed with no response. Our team became concerned about the approaching deadline and decided to combine Knowledge and Green as an alternate solution. However, toward the end of the third week, we received this very concise fax with no elaboration:

> *"Mr. Fain,*
> *We like the 'Good Life City.'*
> *Sincerely, City of Shanghai"*

Shanghai can hardly be unique in this desire. But what is this "good life?" We imagined and presented it as a life that balances work and leisure, with indoor-outdoor living, informality and creativity, health and wellness. Supported by a foundation of knowledge institutions and industries and a framework of green infrastructure, it became the winning proposal for the competition.

This desire for the good life is familiar. Los Angeles once promised it to the world, promoted by compelling imagery like John Van Hamersveld's *Endless Summer* poster from the 1960s advertising the beach lifestyle and iconic worship of sunny outdoor living, sports and fun. Beach Boys anyone?

Compared to the East Coast, L.A. was the epitome of informality; new residents and visitors seemed to leave their baggage behind. My friend John Freeman worked in the White House in the 1970s. On his first trip to California, he boarded a plane in his three-piece suit only to be greeted at LAX by five federal officials in Levi's, open shirts, sandals and gold chains. After a five-day workshop, John had fully adapted to L.A., exchanging his suit for casual clothes. He left L.A. for San Francisco and another week of meetings. After disembarking at the San Francisco airport in his newly acquired Southern California attire, he was greeted by five federal officials in three-piece suits. L.A. was one of a kind, a place that shed its buildings like old clothes. Ed Ruscha's *The Los Angeles County Museum on Fire* alludes to giving up the old for the new. Both his and David Hockney's work embodied this spirit with alluring imagery. The benign Mediterranean climate, complete with sunshine in January and the possibility of a new life of prosperity and freedom, drew countless people to L.A. throughout the twentieth century. It was the "new-new thing," a place that belonged to the future.

That future has come and gone—the good life could not sustain itself. Today, few people perceive L.A. as a promised land. Due to urbanization and increases in population density, it now has the reputation for being one of the most traffic-choked cities in the U.S. Smog has become synonymous with L.A. With a disproportionately small amount of public space per population, its iconic beaches are now overrun. Fires and landslides plague its overbuilt hills. Racial tension, gang violence and the occasional riot mark its streets; its "peace" officers have developed a reputation for brutality. Its rivers are channelized and forgotten, collectors of trash. It may be for these reasons that many Hollywood disaster movies take pleasure in the destruction of L.A., such as the recent Oscar-winning short film *Logorama*, *Battle: Los Angeles* or the blockbuster *2012*, which respectively destroyed and sank the city into the Pacific Ocean.

But in reality, L.A. still has great potential to offer a good life again. It is a vital and thriving metropolis that retains its foundations for a high quality of life shared by all. Jane Jacobs championed the inherent potential of such large cities when she wrote in *The Death and Life of Great American Cities:* "Big cities have difficulties in abundance, because they have people in abundance. But vital cities are not helpless to combat even the most difficult of problems. They are not passive victims of chains

07

Jane Jacobs, *The Death and Life of Great American Cities* (New York: Vintage Book, 1992), 447-448.

08

Los Angeles Economic Development Corporation. *Los Angeles County Profile.* http://laedc.org/reports.

09

See Appendix, Figures 2a, 2b.

of circumstances, any more than they are the malignant opposite of nature… Dull, inert cities, it is true, do contain the seeds of their own destruction and little else. But lively, diverse, intense cities contain the seeds of their own regeneration, with energy enough to carry over for problems and needs outside themselves." [07]

Lively, diverse, intense… L.A. is all of these, softened by a mild climate that sparks envy across the nation. Its media and creative industries, as well as its universities and other institutions of higher education, are paralleled by only a few cities in the world. Its powerful, diverse and adaptable economy has proven resilient, making L.A. the nation's largest industrial metropolis in terms of employment for most of the past fifty years.[08] The natural landscape of the city, while not as pristine as it was one hundred years ago, has not vanished, and is slowly being reclaimed by dedicated grass roots organizations like Friends of the L.A. River. Feelings of openness and opportunity and the promise of a role in this diverse economy still bring people to L.A. from far and wide.

If any profession should be a champion of the shared good life, it is urban design. Its creation depends upon an improved environment and greater citizen participation. Our professional challenge is: How can we contribute to the prosperity, environmental quality and functioning of our city? What urban designers can do is find physical planning solutions that benefit both the public and private sectors. In so doing, urban designers can support a multitude of economic, social and cultural opportunities, the kind that make a city magical and innovative.

We can creatively design spaces for public enjoyment and engagement in the city. In the 1996 "Greenways Plan for Greater Los Angeles," we proposed using abandoned or under-utilized utility rights-of-way for bike paths and recreation features.[09] The seeds are beginning to germinate in the L.A. River Revitalization Master Plan and in newly formed parks such as Taylor Yard, Los Angeles State Historic Park, or The Cornfield, and the new jogging path around Silver Lake reservoir. We can advocate for public transit, pedestrian connectivity and bicycle use by means of street design and land use strategies. We can make room for public gathering spaces, such as the plan for downtown's Grand Avenue where people from all parts of the city will be able to mix.

Unfortunately, we as urban designers have marginalized our potential role by having too narrow a focus. With increased pressure from the private sector and diminishing leadership from the public sector, we have designed city places that are isolating, car-dominated and unfriendly to the public. In greater L.A., we have failed in our well-meaning attempts to balance private and public interests, resulting in city forms that sequester the Good Life into protected enclaves that merely mimic true civic life.

Edward W. Soja, a professor of the Univeristy of California, Los Angeles and writer on planning and urbanism, argues that urban designers need to advocate for "more democratic, multicultural and socially and spatially-just city-building processes." He makes clear that, "the theory and practice of urban design need not explore the full complexity of this evolving multi-scalar spatial configuration, but at the very least it should not close itself off from it, especially at a time when cities all over the world are experiencing an extraordinary reconfiguration arising in large part from extra-urban forces such as globalization." [10]

New York urban designer Michael Sorkin asserts that without a broadened outlook, urban design might become irrelevant to city-building. "Urban design needs to grow beyond its narrowly described fixation on the 'quality' of life to include its very possibility. This will require a dramatically broadened approach… enhancing equity and diversity and making a genuine contribution to the survival of the planet… Cities… must help rebalance a world of growing polarities between overdevelopment and underdevelopment."[11] In order to keep our profession alive and to play a part in providing millions of people with the opportunity to live the Good Life they wish for, urban designers need to "step up to the plate"— but if we do, will there be business and civic leaders willing to pitch

[10]
Edward W. Soja, "Designing the Postmetropolis," *Harvard Design Magazine* (Fall 2006/Winter 2007): 45.

[11]
Michael Sorkin, "The End(s) of Urban Design," *Harvard Design Magazine* (Fall 2006/Winter 2007): 18.

02

Ed Ruscha, *Los Angeles*
County Museum on Fire,
1968. Oil on canvas,
53-1/2" x 133-1/2".
Courtesy Gagosian Gallery.

David Hockney, *Portrait of an Artist (Pool with Two Figures)*, 1972. Acrylic on canvas, 84" x 120". © David Hockney, Photo Credit: Steven Sloman.

the ball? While we must take responsibility for improving Los Angeles and other cities, we are just one of the players in the vast ball field of the city. Urban designers can offer equitable spatial and land-use solutions, but there must also be societal demand for such spaces.

Many people take part in building and changing the city, piece by piece. More often than not, the players are motivated by self-interest rather than a comprehensive vision of a greater city. As citizens, whether we are builders, investors, regulators, workers or retirees, we need to form a collective vision of what the good life can and should be in Los Angeles. We may often disagree on how to implement our vision, but we can at least bring a range of solutions to the proverbial table that will offer meaningful benefits for everyone. Plazas and parks can only do so much. But if we each resolve to participate—whether citizens, city-builders or urban designers—we can certainly create a good life.

03

WHOEVER DIES WITH THE MOST TOYS WINS

Bumper sticker seen in West L.A.

Consumerism is so enmeshed in our daily lives that it is difficult to see its pervasiveness. The rare moments when we escape it reveal to us the enormity and subtlety of our everyday consumerism. A number of years ago, upon returning from a fellowship in England, I was overwhelmed by the "in your face" marketing bombardment on American television after a year of occasionally watching state-run BBC programming. From cartoon figures bouncing around the screen to the absurd characters trying to get a laugh, every image seemed to be promoting a product or a purchasable lifestyle. I never forgot the contrast between these two very different uses of airwaves. I recall my shock now in light of the difficulties we face in adjusting our insatiable appetite for consumer goods and the natural resources that enable them, such as gasoline, pulp, water and natural land area. Designers are very much a part of this value system overrun by consumerism, and in particular, it is important for us to reflect on this not only as designers but also as Angelenos. Los Angeles, built largely on post-World War II growth and plugged into the "tube," reflects many of the issues facing us today in our consumer culture. In light of this, as both urban designers and citizens, we need to take a closer look and reevaluate our behavior.

Socio-economists say that consumptive behavior is driven by want and need. However, the line between want and need is blurry at best. In the 1950s and 1960s, it was a matter of keeping up with the Joneses down the street. Today, it has evolved to mimicking the "lifestyles of the rich and famous," or as *New York Times* columnist David Brooks calls them, "Bobos"—Bourgeois-Bohemians—in his social critique *Bobos in*

04

12
David Brooks, *Bobos in Paradise: The New Upper Class and How They Got There* (New York: Simon & Schuster, 2000): 102.

13
Richard H. Robbins, *Global Problems and the Culture of Capitalism* (Boston: Allyn and Bacon, 1999): 18-19, quoted in "Creating the Consumer," by Anup Shah in *Global Issues* (www.globalissues.org), May 14, 2003.

14
ibid., 210.

15
Associated Press. "Too much seasonal spirit: Abu Dhabi hotel 'regrets' £7m Christmas tree," *Guardian.co.uk*, December 19, 2010.

16
Allan Wheatley, "China's golden age of consumption," *Reuters*, December 9, 2010. Retrieved online in the *Financial Post*: under subheading "Moonlight Clan."

Paradise. Bobos represent the ironic tendencies of the current consumer class, who "take the quintessential bourgeois activity, shopping, and turn it into quintessential bohemian activities: art, philosophy, social action."[12] Since most Bobos are of the generation that actively questioned the corporate profit agenda and rising mass consumerism in American society in the sixties (two related trends that were promoted by federal agencies like the Department of Commerce[13]), the about-face is startling. What happened to them? They quickly realized that to become part of mainstream society, one must become a consumer.

The "consumer revolution" that established this state of affairs was a by-product of the better-known Industrial Revolution, where "…new technologies had resulted in production of more goods, but there were not enough people to buy them… [but] society quickly adapted to the crisis by convincing people to buy things…"[14]

INVENTION IS THE MOTHER OF NECESSITY

Thorstein Veblen

The result is our "buy now, pay later" culture, a culture that is swiftly spreading around the world, as indicated in the recent controversy over the Christmas tree decorated with expensive jewelry at an Abu Dhabi hotel, which apparently cost the hotel nearly eleven million dollars.[15] Another indicator is the rising class of young urban residents in China who feel quite comfortable with a high-consumption, low-savings lifestyle— they belong to what is called in China the "Moonlight Clan," young adults who regularly spend their entire monthly salary on things considered to be luxury items just one generation ago.[16]

GOD FORBID THAT INDIA SHOULD EVER TAKE TO INDUSTRIALISM AFTER THE MANNER OF THE WEST... IF [OUR NATION] TOOK TO SIMILAR ECONOMIC EXPLOITATION, IT WOULD STRIP THE WORLD BARE LIKE LOCUSTS.

Mahatma Gandhi

17 Juliet Schor, "The New Politics of Consumption: Why Americans want so much more than they need," (*Boston Review,* Summer 1999): 10th paragraph under subheading "The New Consumerism."

People are so focused on matching the lifestyle they have been programmed to expect that few resources are left for anything else. Juliet Schor, professor of sociology at Boston College, writes, "That is arguably what happened in the 1980s and 1990s: resources shifting into private consumption, and away from free time, the public sector and savings. Hours of work have risen dramatically, savings rates have plummeted, public funds for education, recreation and the arts have fallen in the wake of grass-roots tax revolt."[17] All of this energy is focused by a "me-me" generation for whom private gain is more valuable than quality public services and more livable cities.

18

Dave Tilford, *Why Consumption Matters,* (Dave Tilford, 2000): under the subheading "The Consumer Class."

19

ibid., 4th paragraph under the subheading "The Consumer Class."

WHAT IS THE USE OF A HOUSE IF YOU HAVEN'T GOT A TOLERABLE PLANET TO PUT IT ON?

Henry David Thoreau

In addition to diverting financial resources from shared services and amenities, inflated spending habits are destroying the environment. Indicators of this destruction are everywhere. It is said that the high-end "consumer class" that represents 20 percent of the world's population (United States, Europe, Japan and Australia) consumes annually 86 percent of the world's consumed resources. The U.S. alone, with only 5 percent of the world's population, consumes 22 percent of the world's fossil fuel production and creates 24 percent of the world's carbon dioxide emissions. [18] "A child born in the United States will create 13 times as much ecological damage over the course of his or her lifetime than a child born in Brazil."[19] Yet the world marketplace continues to emulate the United States; they want what we have, the seemingly good life. We are already consuming beyond the earth's ecological carrying capacity. If everyone in the world used as many resources as we do, it would take four additional Earths to provide the same goods and services. Clearly, our habits have to change—enough is enough.

A MAN IS RICH IN PRO-PORTION TO THE NUMBER OF THINGS HE CAN AFFORD TO LET ALONE.

Henry David Thoreau

"We're not certain why they disappeared, but archeologists speculate that it may have had something to do with their size."

As architects and urban designers, we can only play a supporting role in addressing the global trend of excessive consumerism. Nonetheless, I would propose that our professions adopt goals such as the following that will help us and our cities move in a healthier direction:

1—Redefine a good life that is rooted in public benefit, not just in private gratification. Design and plan urban environments that offer and promote real alternatives to shopping. Imagine public spaces that are not completely dominated and controlled by surrounding retail, but also include multiple uses like libraries, recreational centers and community gardens that make way for drop-in basketball games, Tai Chi or chess in the park. Work with the city to develop and promote programs for people to contribute to the well-being of the city as a whole, as an alternative to buying a new television.

2—Promote shared transportation systems that economically utilize energy and lure people out of private automobiles and into more environmentally sound alternatives. Create opportunities in every development for pedestrians and bike use. Develop smarter and more energy- and water-efficient buildings, neighborhoods and cities. Increase the city's material recycling and reuse industries.

3—As a profession, reward design that is truly innovative and responsible, rather than merely fashionable. Industry leaders can set the example, using their influence to promote buildings and communities with truly beneficial qualities. Students and professionals alike are deeply influenced by the priorities set by the profession.

4—Educate ourselves and our clients about building an urban environment using materials and methods creatively for the long-term benefit of our communities and planet. As unpopular as the topic of "consumption" is today, its implications need to become a greater part of our industry's discourse in universities, "think-tanks" and the press.

Designers are inventors who live within a consumer paradigm. We invented the modern shopping mall and the cul-de-sac. We are not only shapers, but also consumers of the built environment, and of the un-built if you count the ecological footprint of our cities in air quality and waste management, which extend far beyond the limits of the city itself. From this vantage point, we have a unique opportunity to lead by example, informed by our professional knowledge and training.

WHAT SCALE IS APPROPRIATE? IT DEPENDS ON WHAT WE ARE TRYING TO DO. THE QUESTION OF SCALE IS EXTREMELY CRUCIAL TODAY, IN POLITICAL, SOCIAL, AND ECONOMIC AFFAIRS JUST AS IN ALMOST EVERYTHING ELSE.

E.F. Schumacher [20]

[20]
E.F. Schumacher, *Small is Beautiful: Economics as if People Mattered*, 1999 edition, (Point Roberts, WA: Hartley & Marks, 1999): 49.

Shortly after Richard Weinstein moved to Los Angeles to become Dean of UCLA's School of Architecture and Urban Planning in 1983, he talked about his impressions of Los Angeles. Weinstein had worked in New York City's Urban Design Group in the 1970s, and the comparisons he made between New York and L.A. were pointed. He stated that urban development in L.A. was made up of a series of large "organs" connected by "arteries" within the "mulch" of the city. The image of large-scale organs such as shopping centers, marts and downtown redevelopment and the small-scale mulch of single-family homes, dingbat apartments, neighborhood retail and small industries resonated.

Though small and large are both driving forces behind this mulch-organ landscape, much of our city has been shaped by large financial deals, in which "place entrepreneurs" transformed the city to capture urban activity. This can be seen throughout L.A.'s development, from the early conversion of farmland into subdivisions by families like the Chandlers to government-assisted consolidated private developments at what former L.A. Planning Director Calvin Hamilton called "centers."[21] These city-changing developments are enabled by large capital formations, where money pooled by financial institutions, government agencies and private investors is lent to entrepreneurs to fund immense new developments. These projects are often accompanied by large land assemblages.

Because of the need to profit from such large projects, developers try to trap all activity within their project boundaries, reorganizing urban space in order to "shift internal costs of activities to other areas or to others in their own area, and to capture the benefits of those activities, particularly rents, for themselves."[22] What often results are isolated worlds within a city, large swaths of urban land completely controlled by a single owner. Projects that have an objective to concentrate activity, thereby realizing economies in the scale of operation, often lead to self-containment that ignores and separates itself from the surrounding city context and discourages opportunities for civic interaction. *This is big stand-alone architecture, and big stand-alone architecture is not urban design.* If not designed properly, they create irreversible damage to the form of the city. Jane Jacobs labeled such projects as lifeless and rotting, noting, "A new corpse is laid out. It does not smell yet, but it is just as dead, just as incapable of the constant adjustments, adaptations and permutations that make up the processes of life."[23]

The purpose of this essay, however, is not to call for an end to large, private development projects in cities. Healthy cities require these just as much as they require small developments and enterprises. City governments need to recognize the need for both large and small and work to accommodate

[21] Refers to various activity centers throughout Los Angeles selected for higher density development as outlined in Los Angeles Planning Department's "1970 Concept Los Angeles: The Concept for Los Angeles General Plan."

[22] John R. Logan and Harvey L. Molotch, *Urban Fortunes: The Political Economy of Place*, (Los Angeles: University of California Press, 1987): 34.

[23] Jacobs, *Death and Life*, 199.

types of regulation and assistance. In particular, because of the size and nature of big developments, they stand to have a much greater impact on their immediate surroundings and the city-region at large. Therefore, their land uses and physical qualities (their planning and design) require much greater scrutiny by city and community leaders. This may seem like an obvious point, but countless built projects show that it is not.

24
See Appendix, Figure 3.

David Hockney, *Hancock St., West Hollywood*, 1, 1989. Oil on canvas 16 1/2" x 10 1/2", © David Hockney.

When the Pacific Design Center (PDC) was built in the early 1970s in what is now West Hollywood, the plan was to create a shopping mall for the interior design/furniture trade. The "critical mass" project was intended to capture business in an air-conditioned environment in which convenience and economies of scale would profit the industry. Its physical impact was enormous. Architect Cesar Pelli, then at Gruen Associates, understood the project's "object" potential and skillfully designed the glistening blue glass structure and its green and red counterparts with a Melrose Avenue address. Isolated from the sidewalk on Melrose by a gargantuan setback and a blank glass façade, it unapologetically breaks the continuum of storefronts on this popular shopping street, divorcing those businesses to the west of the PDC from those to the east. Although creating an intriguing skyline, the project's urban design is deadly to the continuity of street life. [24]

Given award-winning designers, experienced developers and city officials, how do such important projects like the PDC go awry in this way? I believe that the answer lies not only in the desire for control that often accompanies immense capital formation, but also the veneration of "bigness" by the design team. Many architects glorify big form-making at the expense of the scale and activity of the neighborhood.

Instead, architects need to design large projects to fit into a city's "time-form"—a term artist Bill Viola coined for emergent contextual patterns—and accommodate a wide range of daily interactions, as characterized by Jennifer Lee in her book *Civility in the City*. It is simply a matter of planning and design that determines whether a large project becomes

25
These ideas are explored
in the chapters "Time-Form"
and "Crash."

26
Peter Davey, "Berlin—
Potsdamer Platz
development," *Architecture
Review*, January 1998: under
subheading "Reinterpreting
the European ideal."

an exceptional city and community asset or a life-sucking leviathan. How bigness is inserted into the city determines whether it becomes a benefit or a problem. [25]

The redevelopment of Potsdamer Platz in Berlin exemplifies two distinctly different approaches to bigness side-by-side in an urban setting. After the Berlin Wall was dismantled, a vast barren expanse was left in what was once the heart of the city. Large corporations such as Daimler-Benz (now Daimler AG), Sony and two others had purchased large swaths of this area from the city for redevelopment. Daimler purchased 18.5 acres and Sony 6.5 acres, an area that had once housed a great variety of landowners amidst a rich street network. The city-chosen Hilmer & Sattler redevelopment master plan attempted to recreate the intricate scale of Potsdamer Platz's historic fabric (angering jury member Rem Koolhaas, who famously stormed out of the session); however, the new landowners wanted more. Daimler and Sony both held competitions for their own sites, Daimler choosing a plan by Renzo Piano and Sony a plan by Helmut Jahn. [26]

The two resulting projects couldn't be more different. Whereas Jahn's design for Sony internalizes the project circulation into an American-like mall, Piano divides the Daimler property into multiple parcels, defined by a network of public streets and plazas. The resulting Sony Center simply glorifies big architecture. In the end, Sony's property completely disregarded Hilmer & Sattler's plan, choosing Jahn's private commercial complex of eight buildings (all designed by Jahn) with no public through-streets or real public spaces. It is essentially 1.4 million square feet of monotonous super-block, without any diversity or relief. Ironically, architects laud the project as a great accomplishment of modern architecture. The Daimler project, requiring just as much government and private financial resources, fits much more comfortably into its setting. Piano's plan greatly increases the intensity of the site (5.3 million square feet), but remains the truest to Hilmer & Sattler's plan of through-streets and public spaces. The new blocks were divided amongst six different architects to create a richer and more diverse urban fabric. Multiple uses and the buildings' pedestrian orientation facilitate a revival of street life in Potsdamer Platz.[27]

Koolhaas, who took offense at the modest urban scale of the Hilmer & Sattler plan, is a contemporary spokesperson for "bigness." He celebrates it in commentaries like S, M, L, XL and in his own design practice, as in the mammoth China Central Television (CCTV) building in Beijing. In his book, Delirious New York, Koolhaas describes Raymond Hood's 1929 theoretical plan for Manhattan ("Manhattan 1950") as his inspiration for such large-scale interventions. Hood's vision proposed greatly intensified developments at key arterial intersections of Manhattan—these developments appear from Hood's sketch drawings to be mega-buildings of huge proportion and scale. Koolhaas identifies these giant developments as the proper vision for the future metropolis.[28] Ironically, he diverges from Hood in the actual way that Hood's Manhattan plan was physically manifested as a responsible and genuine Manhattan development: the Rockefeller Center.

The Rockefeller Center epitomizes how an enormous project can be a city asset. It is still "the largest privately-owned building enterprise ever undertaken in the U.S."[29] This "city within a city" would have been the fifty-first largest city in the U.S. at the time of its completion in 1939. What Hood, John D. Rockefeller, Jr., and their team accomplished was the masterful integration of large-scale private land use and a human-scaled urban environment. The original Rockefeller Center broke up its massive 5 million square feet into block-size development phases, multiple buildings and public activities integrated into the street space. Hood scaled his highest tower in a series of steps, the lowest of which aligns with the older brownstones of the neighborhood. As Jacobs points out, its extra north-south street, which breaks through the long mid-town blocks, makes it a center of use, mixing paths, points of contact and public

27
See Appendix, Figure 4.

28
Rem Koolhaas, Delirious New York: A Retroactive Manifesto for Manhattan" (New York: Monacelli Press, 1994): in the Chapter "How Perfect Perfection Can Be: The Creation of Rockefeller Center," 161-207.

29
Great Public Spaces Article "Rockefeller Center" in the Project for Public Spaces (www.pps.org).

30

Jacobs, *Death and Life*, 182.

31

Rockefeller Center
Website, "Art and
History," copyrighted by
Tishman Speyer (www.
rockefellercenter.com).

32

See Appendix, Figure 5.

33

See Appendix, Figure 6.

interaction. [30] From the time of its opening, the development invited the public to embrace it. To this end, Hood made Rockefeller Center simultaneously into a commercial center and social hub by breaking down the scale, maintaining public accessibility and providing civic amenities. Even during its nine-year construction, it benefited the city by directly and indirectly employing an estimated 40,000 workers during the Great Depression. [31] Rockefeller Center was unprecedented, and remains a successful and beloved part of Manhattan. [32]

By contrast, Koolhaas' highly touted 6-million-square-foot CCTV project cannot be called a true city asset. His project's bigness seems intended to intimidate rather than benefit the public. Unlike Hood's Rockefeller Center, Koolhaas totally disregards the project setting within Beijing's Central Business District and appears to be consumed by the internalized aspects of this large-scale highly secured complex. The project ignores open space networks and other public through ways prescribed by the city's plan that would have connected the site to other parts of the district and creates a media hub that symbolizes dominance and control. [33]

Cities have the responsibility to encourage large developments to be designed according to public benefit. This may not have been possible in Beijing because of the government's desire for control, but it is certainly possible in the West. One excellent example of this is the Bo01 development in Malmö, Sweden. Bo01 was the 60-acre, 1.9-million-square-foot first phase of the redevelopment of Malmö's Western Harbor industrial waterfront area. From the start, the city set out to create a diverse, vibrant and sustainable mixed-use neighborhood. Instead of one or two large developers, the city invited many developers of different sizes to participate in Bo01's planning and building. They collaboratively established a unique block plan for the site, which was further broken down into parcels and divided among the developers. Ultimately, eighteen developers and twenty-two architects joined the city in making this celebrated redevelopment. In a case study, the German

Transportation Agency observed, "It questions the approach of large-scale uniformed [sic] development solutions and proves that small-scale varied packages are both financially achievable and arguably more profitable in the long run."[34] It takes desire, willingness and patience from the developers and architects to work together and accomplish this type of development. I am not certain you would witness such cooperation in the development and architectural community in Los Angeles. The Malmö project, nevertheless, possesses a very high degree of variety and a superior level of creativity.[35]

As Los Angeles becomes denser with ever-larger projects, questions of neighborhood "fit" and reasonable human scale loom to the forefront. E.F. Schumacher, who wrote the seminal economic treatise *Small is Beautiful*, expounded the profound meaning of this challenge of scale: "What is the meaning of democracy, freedom, human dignity, standard of living, self-realization, fulfillment? Is it a matter of goods, or of people? Of course it is a matter of people. But people can be themselves only in small comprehensible groups. Therefore we must learn to think in terms of an articulated structure that can cope with a multiplicity of small-scale units. If economic thinking cannot grasp this it is useless."[36] With regard to the future, the City of Los Angeles needs carefully crafted, specific plans and land-use regulations that will address these issues. The recently drafted Arroyo Seco-Cornfield Specific Plan and the Grand Avenue Project offer excellent opportunities to accommodate both large and small developments. Does the development community have the will?

[34] German Federal Ministry of Transport, Building and Urban Affairs, "Shipyards to Sustainability: Bo01/Mälmo/Sweden," "Baukulture" as an Impulse for Growth: Good Examples for European Cities, April 2007: 15.

[35] See Appendix, Figures 7a, 7b.

[36] Schumacher, *Small is Beautiful*, 56.

ILLUMINATION

07

Sigfried Giedion observed that, "...in the history of architecture, city planning—urban design—has been a late comer in every period. Usually several centuries were needed before a period became *ripe* enough... City Planning [Urban Design] blossoms when the way of life of a period has become so self-evident that it can be immediately translated into plans." [37] Implicit in this statement is that urban design is not a constant. Urban design is a complex way of organizing that only emerges when a society has reached a certain level of maturity. We experienced a "ripening" such as this during the 1960s and 1970s, when there was a proliferation of illuminated thinking about city making.

Many of us are familiar with the great writers and practitioners of that time: Christopher Alexander's essay "A City is not a Tree," Jane Jacobs' *The Death and Life of Great American Cities*, E.F. Schumacher's *Small* is *Beautiful*, and Ian McHarg's *Design with Nature*, among others. Each brought a new way of understanding a city as a collection of complex interactions—social, economical and environmental—that evolve over time. Although techniques have become more sophisticated, many of the fundamental principles emerged during this period.

Perhaps the most provocative article written in the 1960s was Melvin Webber's, "Planning in an Environment of Change." Webber not only called for the design of cities in more complex ways, but also provided a strategy through which to do this called "permissive planning." In this approach, plans are open-ended, less architectural and more process-driven, sensitive to market conditions and to issues of equity, and are planned for diversity. Permissive planning called for new methods of public participation with less direction from "higher authorities" in the planning and design of cities.

Webber prophetically wrote: "During the next decades, planning is likely to become the normal mode of deciding and acting in a wide array of societal affairs. At the same time, we shall be living with increasing affluence, increasing relative poverty, and increasing power in the hands of the few technically proficient planners. It will then be all the more necessary that decisions be guided by the outputs of government actions, *outputs* measured by their welfare benefits to the plurality of publics who will inhabit the post-industrial society. The concepts and methods that emerged during the early days of the industrial age are not likely to suit us in the post-industrial age. Now, and increasingly in the future, the hard decisions will have to rely upon explicit statements in the wants of the publics."[38]

Although these ideas were challenging at the time of their initiation, they have become an integral part of city planning today. In 1970s England, they became the philosophical underpinning of a radically different new town called Milton Keynes.[39] In New York City they manifested as incentive zoning, resulting in innovative planning

[38]
Melvin M. Webber, "Planning in an Environment of Change, Part 2: Permissive Planning." *Town Planning Review* 39(4): 295.

[39]
Webber's ideas were responding to the British New Town program, which up to that time had promoted fixed, radial planning solutions such as at Cumbernauld, Scotland. His writings greatly influenced Richard Llewelyn-Davies as he devised the master plan for the new town Milton Keynes, resulting in a non-hierarchical, open-ended grid of streets emphasizing "opportunity and freedom of choice." (Milton Keynes Development Corporation, *The Plan for Milton Keynes*, March 1970.)

40
Jerold S. Kayden, The
Department of City Planning
of the City of New York and
The Municipal Art Society of
New York. *Privately Owned
Public Space: The New York
City Experience.* (New York
2009: John Wiley & Sons,
Inc.): 1.

41
Barnett, *Public Policy,* 66-67.

mechanisms such as the "Special Purpose District," invented by New York City's Urban Design Group in the late 1960s. Unique urban design policies were crafted to address each district's specific issues. The districts used a combined "carrot and stick" approach. Mandatory provisions, particularly having to do with land uses and setbacks, were prescribed in the zoning ordinance. Elective provisions allowing for floor to area ratio (FAR) bonuses were made accountable by identifying improvements for specific locations in the physical plan. Each district's plan anticipated city requirements and allowed individual properties to be redeveloped as-of-right. Public priorities were established and then codified to encourage development choices appropriate to those priorities and discourage those that were not. While these and other elements of New York's incentive zoning policies were fine-tuned over the years, they were, as described by Harvard planning and law professor Jerold S. Kayden, "one of the most effective demonstrations of the law's power to promote specific design outcomes."[40] Urban design was no longer dependent on public entrepreneurs like Ed Logue or Robert Moses.

These special policy frameworks help the city protect public interest, while permitting private developers to act creatively to fulfill their own aims. This allows for a valuable diversity of spaces, facilities and structures within a community. "The city government seeks to define only those elements of concern to the public, leaving the developer to operate as he will within these clearly stated constraints. The elements of the plan are tied back into the pre-existing fabric," explains Jonathan Barnett in *Urban Design as Public Policy.* "At the same time, the nature of the design controls permits the design to make sense as each increment is added; and they are sufficiently flexible to allow for modifications as time goes on." [41]

Permissive planning has also been used to innovate the nonprofit sector. Massachusetts Institute of Technology professor Don Terner pioneered the application of permissive planning philosophy into real world urban needs. In 1974, he started a nonprofit organization in New York that converted abandoned buildings into usable community assets and safe affordable housing. The organization, called the Urban Homesteading Assistance Board (UHAB), has been hugely successful and still operates today. What was so unique about UHAB's agenda was that they convinced lower-income urban residents, including street gangs like the Harlem Renegades, as well as the city government to cooperate in recycling abandoned residential buildings. Urban residents learned specialized skills in carpentry, plumbing, finance, group organization, building management and other technical training as they worked on a city-donated building. "Sweat equity" was born. Terner and UHAB created a process that substituted labor for capital, redeveloping whole communities with a participatory process.

The permissive planning process that allowed limited-equity cooperatives was a revolutionary method to solve a big problem, the discord between a supply of abandoned, decaying housing and an enormous demand for lower-income housing. Over the course of thirty-plus years that UHAB has been facilitating such cooperatives (co-ops), the results have been very positive. In terms of equity, quality of life, community building and stabilizing the lives of vulnerable lower-income citizens, this participatory method has proved vastly superior to traditional top-down approaches to public housing.

A report on a low-income housing survey done by Susan Saegert, a professor of environmental psychology at the City University of New York, revealed that, "Co-ops had the best building service, the fewest 'poor' ratings, the best repair quality and management characteristics and the fewest problems with crime and drugs. Co-op residents generally described their housing positively and were more likely to want to stay in their apartments. Co-op members had higher levels of civic participation and were more likely to be involved in tenant organizations." [42]

[42] The report is discussed in Neil F. Carlson, *UHAB Comes of Age: Thirty Years of Self-Help Housing in New York* (New York: UHAB, 2004).

43
The report is discussed in
Neil F. Carlson, *UHAB Comes
of Age: Thirty Years of Self-
Help Housing in New York*
(New York: UHAB, 2004): 9.

Creating permissive planning frameworks such as self-help housing will never be the easiest route for cities to take. It is always easier for authorities to make all decisions, especially when the group they serve has little political voice, but these top-down approaches rarely create the healthy communities that cities desperately need. New York housing activist Harry DeRienzo explains, "It's really hard work. I mean it's easy to go to a big developer and say, 'Look, let's knock down all the buildings, let's build up new partnership housing, and screen the tenants, and market the units, and rent them out.' That's easy development. The hard development is working building by building with tenants in place, training them. It's labor-intensive. It's hard. But in the end that's how you build community." [43]

These varied applications of permissive planning have had a profound impact on planning cities today. In my own work, the model has inspired me to create urban design frameworks that are deferential to others, where progress will be measured by the ability of these systems to allow others to act. As designers of the city, we can understand from Webber's thesis that actual pluralism in urban design is the creation of circumstances in which many others can express themselves. However, one finds many misinterpretations of this thesis, particularly with large-scale, architecturally driven master plans, which are a sort of prescriptive planning. As practitioners we need to have the courage to explore the difference between these two approaches so that we don't fall into the hole of prescriptive planning but find illumination through a permissive alternative.

URBAN INFRASTRUCTURE

44
Craig Owens, *History of Century City*, Century City Chamber of Commerce website (www.centurycitycc. com): 4th paragraph under the subheading "The Big Sale."

45
Ibid., 3rd paragraph under the subheading "Welton Becket – Master Architect."

46
See Appendix, Figures 8a, 8b.

In 1960, national developer Bill Zeckendorf called a meeting of the nation's top architects and urban planners to plan a new Los Angeles neighborhood, Century City. Known for his large-scale urban renewal type projects at L'Enfant Plaza in Washington D.C. and his housing project at Kips Bay in Manhattan, Zeckendorf, in partnership with Aluminum Company of America,[44] brought together a team led by local architect Welton Becket that included I.M. Pei, Minoru Yamasaki, Pietro Belluschi and Frederick J. Gebers.[45] Twentieth Century Fox Studios had made the decision that its studio backlot near Beverly Hills had become too valuable to remain in use for movie production. The purpose of the meeting was to conceptualize a "new city" based on a different approach to infrastructure and urban planning. The concept, which we see built today, was intentionally developed by the creative team as a striking contrast to the old downtown Los Angeles.[46] The old downtown was viewed as inefficient, congested, dirty and served by infrastructure that reflected an outdated way of life that promoted pedestrian movement, transit and mixed use. The "new" paradigm, as they saw it, was clean, efficient, spacious and based upon the "wonders" of the automobile. Since Los Angeles' 1100-mile Red Car streetcar system had been dismantled in the 1950s, cars and other motor vehicles have dominated the region.

The new project was called a "city within a city," inspired by the term used by the developers of Rockefeller Center thirty years earlier. With the large size of the property, Zeckendorf had an almost completely clean slate to do things differently from the old downtown. With this objective, the new city would be unencumbered by existing congested roadways. Streetcars would no longer be sharing right-of-ways, and buildings would not overshadow and crowd the street. Drawings were made of broad boulevards surrounding immense parcels of land. The layout allowed the driver easy access to the developments and their readily available parking. However, based on the current zoning, an office or retail development would require at least as many square feet of parking as would be permitted for its use. This required the parcels to be large enough to accommodate all of that square footage. This was acceptable, as pedestrian circulation could then be internalized to each parcel and connected where necessary by elevated pedestrian bridges at important junctures. Land usage was laid out without regard for the mix of uses, with the exception of the ABC Center with its Shubert Theater and restaurants (now demolished for yet another single-use office complex) at the heart of Century City on Avenue of the Stars, across from the Century Plaza Hotel.

The new and untested infrastructure of Century City was designed to prioritize car movement. It did not include publicly accessible parks or amenities like schools, libraries and community centers. The retail center was concentrated at one edge as an open-air mall, not at the geographic center of the plan.

Century City was unveiled with an exuberant optimism for the "new" city and a disdain for the "old," but this bold abandonment of the multi-faceted qualities of older urban areas operated under the reckless belief that the car was the only necessary mode of transportation. Today, amidst a reemergence of urban living, people are rediscovering older city neighborhoods as a special resource. People are rejecting long commutes, isolated neighborhoods and characterless suburbs that have resulted from complete automobile orientation. They are learning the value and convenience of a walkable neighborhood. As old downtown Los Angeles seemed out of date in the 1950s, Century City seems so today. It is ironic that many currently desirable living amenities are once again offered in the old downtown. Adaptively reused, the older neighborhood offers convenient access to public transit, cultural facilities, jobs and urban activities that Century City lacks. In new ways, we are moving ahead by going "back to the future."

47
Pierre Belanger, "Redefining Infrastructure," *Ecological Urbanism* (Baden, Switzerland: Lars Müller Publishers, 2010): 344.

48
Mohsen Mostafavi, "Why Ecological Urbanism? Why Now?" *Ecological Urbanism* (Baden, Switzerland: Lars Müller Publishers, 2010): 32-33.

49
Enrique Peñalosa, "Politics, Power, Cities," *The Endless City* (London: Phaidon Press, 2008): 315.

Until now, infrastructure has been the exclusive realm of utilities engineering. We need to expand our definition. The needs of today's networked city are very different from the world Century City was built to serve, and it demands an updated approach. Given today's standards, what should urban infrastructure encompass? It needs to go beyond the approach of Century City-like development, which envisioned only roads and utilities. Today's urban infrastructure must involve a more open-ended and inclusive definition that addresses the public realm, not only roads and utilities, but also public transit, bike ways, publicly accessible open space, libraries, schools, community centers and sustainable environmental processes. Much is at stake. Pierre Belanger asks, "How then can we rethink the conventional logic of infrastructure—the background process of essential services that underlies cities and regions—to effectively sustain sprawling populations and diversify urban economies in the future?"[47] In the same volume, editor Mohsen Mostavi writes, "Because the public sector deals with the operations and maintenance of existing cities, it bears primary responsibility for considering alternative ways of addressing these issues."[48]

Infrastructure affects our democracy and expresses the civility of our nation. The respect for maintaining and expanding appropriate infrastructure is indicative of the value and priority we place on our economy, our culture and our environment. The former mayor of Bogotá, Enrique Peñalosa, explains, "…a government that cares about quality of urban life and democracy has to progressively veer away from trying to reduce traffic jams through investments in new or bigger roads, and instead concentrate on creating and improving mass-transit and pedestrian and bicycle facilities."[49]

Los Angeles urgently needs to renew itself according to a broader and greener vision of infrastructure in order to become more vital, affordable and healthier. In particular, four areas of this retrofit need special attention: mobility and redundant systems, the grid, parks and plazas and functional integration.

08

MOBILITY AND "REDUNDANT" SYSTEMS

The transport and exchange of goods, services and information are central to the form of the city. Congestion is problematic because it delays transactions, dampening economic activity. In MasterCard's Worldwide Centers of Commerce Index conducted in 2007 and 2008, Los Angeles dropped from an international ranking of ten to seventeen, largely because competing cities have developed better urban mobility, reducing congestion.[50] In contrast, the Los Angeles movement system is dominated by the car. Our bus system is among the most extensive in the world, but it is comingled with automobiles, which makes it terribly inefficient. We need to build new modes of conveniently located transport that give our citizens choices of movement.

"Redundant," or multi-modal transportation systems, would greatly benefit Los Angeles. We need to be able to travel on a number of available systems in a timely manner, separated from each other, yet integrated. As Jaime Lerner, the former mayor of Curitiba, Brazil,

08
©Edward Koren, 2/15/1969,
The New Yorker Collection,
www.cartoonbank.com.

50
MasterCard Worldwide,
2008 MasterCard Worldwide Centers of Commerce Index,
June 2008.

51
Jaime Lerner invterviewed
by Zara Bilgrami for
CNN, "Maveric mayor:
'Eco-architecture not ego-
architecture,'" June 6, 2008
(www.cnn.com).

explains, "...don't try to choose which system is best. Use all the systems, but with one condition: never, never compete in the same space [e.g., avoid combining buses and private automobiles in the same movement lanes]. They have to be complementary. So combine all of the systems..."[51] If one system is congested, another system should be available to accommodate movement. Arguments have been made against this, the most common being that L.A. is so spread out that public transit cannot work here. However, in order to be efficient, transit needs its own right-of-way much in the way cars need theirs, too. Meanwhile, we are losing ground to other urban regions, nationally and globally. The economic competitiveness of our region will be affected by how quickly we can move about.

China offers a number of dramatic examples of how cities are being modernized, dramatic because they are moving so quickly to upgrade urban infrastructure. It is amazing to see what can be accomplished in a short period of time. Admittedly, there have been significant social costs resulting from such rapid transformation. We hear stories of the Three Gorges Dam relocation and of entire neighborhoods being relocated to build roads in central Beijing and Shanghai. The rapid expansion of private car ownership has created major congestion problems in Chinese cities while reducing bike usage. It is ironic to see reduced bike usage in cities like Beijing while cities like Paris and London are embracing it. However, it appears that most Chinese sense that progress is being made and that the quality of life is improving. For over fifteen years the Chinese have been committed to upgrading their cities with multiple transport systems: new roadways, subway lines, exclusive bus service, bike ways and regional high speed rail. They understand very clearly that their cities must function efficiently in order to be competitive in a global economy. In the Johnson Fain plan for Beijing's Central Business District, done over ten years ago, we recommended a subway connection from the airport to the business district. It was completed in seven years. An experimental Maglev high-speed elevated train was built in two-and-a-half years between downtown

Shanghai and the airport, a 35 kilometer distance that takes just over seven minutes at a top speed of 430 kilometers per hour. Smaller regional cities like Chengdu and Chongqing have major subway systems under construction.

Perhaps the most ambitious program in China is the planned construction of a high-speed rail system throughout the country, connecting major cities. Rail authorities expect this to be in place within ten years. In California, we have been trying to build a high-speed rail system between Los Angeles and San Francisco for over forty years, but the rights of way are still yet to be acquired.

Developments in mobility infrastructure are inevitably going to affect the way we live; the question is whether they will improve our quality of life. In San Francisco, new carpool tolls have been established on many of the region's bridges, causing 30 percent of motorists to select alternative modes of transportation such as Bay Area Rapid Transit (BART), bus and bicycling.[52] This situation is similar to the proposals for "congestion pricing" in Los Angeles. Whether this will decrease quality of life in the city or not depends on the urban infrastructure in place to accommodate viable alternatives.

GRIDS

Lieutenant E. O. C. Ord surveyed the first plan for Los Angeles in 1849. Ord used a grid plan with Main Street as the edge along the top of the bluff. The plan extended south and wrapped around Bunker Hill to the west. A succession of other grids followed as the city expanded westerly and annexed more unincorporated areas, including those from the Hancock and Hansen surveys of 1853 and 1859. During the 1920s, 1930s and 1940s the county engineers imposed a super-grid road plan based on farm roads and Red Line routes, an organizational pattern that extended into the San Fernando Valley and northern Orange County.

In the 1960s the planning of the Irvine Ranch and similar projects

[52] Will Kane, "Bay Area bridge tolls take a toll on commuters," San Francisco Chronicle, July 29, 2010: A-1.

53
See Appendix, Figures
9a, 9b.

54
See Appendix, Figures
10, 11.

55
See Appendix, Figure 12.

embracing the new development paradigm of private residential enclaves put an end to grids. The traditional grid layouts of the past were abandoned with the onset of the new auto age, when traffic engineers employed hierarchical road systems beginning with cul-de-sac neighborhoods, tertiary, secondary and primary streets. The grid was replaced by a "tree," triggering alarm from some planners and academics such as Christopher Alexander who responded to this trend with the essay, "A City is Not a Tree," written in the late 1960s. Most neighborhoods in Irvine, like Turtle Rock, are designed as private enclaves, and others were later added as gated communities.[53] Their road systems have promoted a suburban lifestyle that is generally isolated from urban interaction and built around the scale of the automobile instead of comfortable walking distances scaled to the pedestrian. It is important to recognize that early Los Angeles was not like this and was more like other traditional cities with gridiron plans.

The grid offers many advantages in organizing a city's plan. Very importantly, it is a structural framework that provides equal access to land as a resource, and consequently becomes an extension of our democracy. It can be used more universally to provide equitable utility and resource distribution and as a method for establishing urban scale.

The grid is adaptable, open-ended and resilient, with a natural redundancy. A grid of streets provides the city with a flexible system of distributing goods and services and redundant routes that enable ease of movement. In the competition for the University of California, San Francisco's Mission Bay Campus, won by Machado and Silvetti Associates, [54] contestant Steven Holl initially declined to accept the overall grid of streets planned for the redevelopment area. However, during his final presentation, he indicated to the jury that although he had tried a number of schemes that "blew out" the grid, he kept coming back to it, recognizing its overriding positive qualities. Ultimately, he used the grid of streets in creative ways to both set off by contrast and to harmonize with his proposed design. [55]

In *Great Streets*, Allan Jacobs compares the road systems of a number of cities. The width of the street and the size and proportion of the city block is central to a discussion of scale, orientation, walkability and economies related to development of land within each respective city. For example, the San Francisco city block is based upon a Spanish unit of measure called the *vara*. A vara is 2.75 feet[56] and the San Francisco's block size is 100 by 150 varas, 275 by 412.5 feet. The size corresponds to a block that is easily navigable as a pedestrian yet still large enough for efficient parking and building layout. At a conservative walking pace of about three miles per hour, a pedestrian covers about 275 feet per minute, making the vara block one by one and one-half minutes in pedestrian dimensions. In comparison the Portland, Oregon block is 200 by 200 feet, a dimension which is very pedestrian friendly, yet difficult for large-scale redevelopment, which may require the assemblage of all parcels of land within the block in order to develop efficiently.[57] Blocks in Midtown Manhattan between Fifth Avenue and 12th Avenue are 200 feet in the north-south direction, a very easy pedestrian distance, yet very long in the east-west direction at approximately 800 feet.[58] In response, the 1971 Fifth Avenue Special Purpose Zoning District provided arcade walkways connecting east-west streets at mid-block.[59]

Although Downtown L.A.'s block is more pedestrian-friendly than an 1100-foot block in Century City, at 350 by 550 feet,[60] it is still too large for easy pedestrian movement. Yet this is not nearly as large as the Orange County block of the Irvine Business Complex (IBC), which varies, but can reach 1200 by 1200 feet,[61] completely disregarding comfortable walking distances.[62] No matter where you go you have to get in the car just to travel a block away. The absurdity of this arrangement has become clear and costly, and cities are trying to transform these car-only environments into something more pedestrian friendly. For example, just south of the IBC is the auto oriented office district of Newport Beach. The city's voters recently passed a zone change referendum allowing for mixed-use, multi-family residential and

[56]
See Appendix, Figure 13.

[57]
See Appendix, Figure 14.

[58]
See Appendix, Figure 15.

[59]
See Appendix, Figures 1a, 1b.

[60]
See Appendix, Figure 8b.

[61]
As measured from the scaled figure-ground block plan of the Irvine Business District in Allan Jacobs' *Great Streets*, page 221.

[62]
See Appendix, Figure 16.

63
See Appendix, Figure 17.

64
See Appendix, Figure 18.

retail. The proposed 24-hour environment will be organized according to pedestrian-scaled spaces and blocks. Implementation of this new zoning will be complicated, given the complex arrangements of existing land holdings and building ownerships, but the city is committed to change because of the benefits of a more finely grained urban environment.

It is interesting to note that in Shanghai's new Pudong Financial District, block sizes are also too large. They are based on U.S. car-dominated analogies.[63] The city is now considering introduction of smaller, more pedestrian-friendly blocks in future developments, following the model of Shanghai's historic PuXi area.[64]

PUBLIC OPEN SPACE

The planning and design of several large commercial office towers for the Blue Cross headquarters site in Warner Center in the early 1990s provided some special challenges to the planning team at Johnson Fain. As the program density increased, roadway and building footprint requirements consumed the limited land area, squeezing out anything but minimal pedestrian and public open space. Concerned that most commercial developments within the city were being confronted with a similar issue, the team asked a simple question: "How much of the city's land area is devoted to public open space?" Serious investigation revealed that Los Angeles lagged far behind other prominent cities in the United States. For example, it was determined that the surface area devoted to public open space in Boston and San Francisco is approximately 9 percent; Seattle, around 13 percent; and New York City at approximately 17 percent.

Even though Los Angeles has Griffith Park, the largest urban park in the U.S., L.A.'s percentage of open public space totaled a mere 4 percent. Sadly, this means that locations of greatest need, i.e., South Central Los Angeles and the Rampart neighborhoods west of downtown, are the worst served. Apartment districts in these neighborhoods typically house large families but have no backyards or outdoor family recreation space, an important necessity that public parks should fulfill. In a visit to Los Angeles in the late 1980s, Paul Goldberger commented that Los Angeles is a very private city. What could have been public space was devoted to private backyards in a city with an overabundance of single-family detached homes.

A movement occurred in the 1930s to increase the prominence and distribution of open public space infrastructure in Los Angeles. The L.A. Chamber of Commerce commissioned the Olmsted brothers to design an extensive park system for the city. Local politics destroyed the project before it could be implemented. Later, in the early 1990s, a similar plan by Johnson Fain called the "Greenways Plan for Los Angeles" was presented to the city. Inspired by our research findings from the Warner Center project, we wanted to create a comprehensive open space plan and strategy that would benefit much of Los Angeles County. The plan is based upon the use of residual open areas, reactivating the many abandoned rail right-of-ways (from the earlier Red Car system), power easements and flood channel right-of-ways, including the Los Angeles River, as public open space connectors. Much has progressed since, such as the planning of the Los Angeles River and the L.A. City General Plan Update of 1994, which adopted many of the proposed greenway routes. In the next decade, we might even see a giant new park weave through the densest parts of Hollywood and span the Hollywood Freeway. Unlike many of the more traditional American cities, Los Angeles never experienced the City Beautiful Movement that occurred at the turn of the twentieth century. Additionally, urban visionaries such as New York City's Robert Moses led the redevelopment of city parks that increased the "civility" of the city. Meanwhile, many of Los Angeles' public space improvements have been great disappointments. Many plazas and open spaces are embedded in private developments that claim to be great additions to the city but are actually mere malls dressed for public usage. The Grove in the Mid-Wilshire District,[65] Universal CityWalk,[66] the Americana at Brand[67] and Nokia Plaza at L.A. Live near Staples Center[68] all claim to have public plazas but each

[65]
See Appendix, Figure 19.

[66]
See Appendix, Figure 20.

[67]
See Appendix, Figure 21.

[68]
See Appendix, Figure 22.

69
Christopher Hawthorne,
"It has no place: Despite
its name, L.A. Live is not
of the city," *Los Angeles
Times*, Architecture Review,
December 03, 2008: 8th
paragraph.

is a captive to surrounding development. The open space is a means to "pick the public's pockets," as a top MCA executive once said of CityWalk. *Los Angeles Times* architecture critic Chris Hawthorne described L.A. Live and its surrounding development as just "another outdoor mall." [69] While public-private partnerships may be necessary, better guidelines are needed to ensure public accessibility to new open spaces. One good rule of thumb is that a public plaza needs to have *at least* two sides facing a public street, two frontages not controlled by the developer.

INTEGRATION

There is no sense in increased mobility options, better street networks and more parks if none of these are integrated with public needs. What is the point of a park if you can't get to it? What is the point of walkable street grids if what faces the sidewalks are only the blank walls of parking structures? What is the point of a new bike route if the bike rider's life is constantly challenged by freeway-like roadways accommodating rapidly moving platoons of cars and long distance travel because of the spread out land uses? What is the point of a new transit line if it stops short of the destination, such as the Metro Green Line, which approaches LAX but does not reach it. L.A. cannot afford to miss the opportunities arising from infrastructure development, and most crucially from integration with land use. The creation of infrastructure that is not integrated with appropriate land uses can create an urban wasteland of alien buildings and pedestrian isolation, as illustrated poignantly by painter Wayne Thiebaud. Similarly, artist Chris Burden's fascinating kinetic sculpture *Metropolis II* embodies this separation.

By integrating land uses with its public realm (both conventionally and creatively), L.A. can cultivate the latent potential in its urban lands. As shown in the Johnson Fain Greenways Plan, even water culverts and once-abandoned rail right-of-ways can become places of new growth in community life and in the economy. Decaying urban voids can

blossom into vibrant parts of a city. With coordinated and context-driven planning, the latent potential in urban lands can be used as a catalyst for wide-reaching benefits. As Belanger writes, "rezoning and redeveloping land generates financial mechanisms necessary for the reclamation of decaying infrastructure and contaminated land."[70] In an interconnected and interdependent environment like the city, success can only be achieved if benefits are shared, not monopolized.

Land-use adjustments need to be informed by specific contexts, so that changes take advantage of key opportunities while at the same time preserving the many cultural and architectural assets of the city. Where infrastructure and land-use changes can alter the character of historic neighborhoods, specific policies should be enacted to protect those areas.

09
Chris Burden, *Metropolis II*, 2011. Photo by Erich Koyama.

70
Belanger, "Redefining Infrastructure," 345.

The built environment must be integrated with climate and ecology, and many individuals and organizations are devoted to this integration for the development of more sustainable cities. At the macro level, institutions like L.A.'s Department of Water and Power are making significant strides in increasing their sources of renewable energy such as solar arrays and wind farms, as well as recycling treated water. At the micro level, individual buildings are becoming increasingly efficient.

Urban designers operate at the juncture between micro and macro realms. Our plans need to support and reinforce both levels, recognizing sun angles, wind, water bodies, flood patterns, soil conditions, ecological habitats, biomass and available resources. How can the infrastructure to replenish groundwater become an open space amenity? How can blocks be shaped to take advantage of natural light for living and working spaces? How can living and working be connected to convenient transit and bike routes? And how can underutilized parcels become community gardens? These are a few examples of environmental issues addressed by the urban designer. Subtle moves can have great impacts. For example, in northern China, street grids are laid out so that buildings receive adequate sunlight in winter months. Ultimately, urban design is the arena in which nature, technology, economy and lifestyle can come together to make a sustainable reality. It is ecological urbanism, an approach that integrates urban infrastructure with life.

CRASH

71
Herman Knoflacher, Philip Rode and Geetam Tiwari, "How Roads Kill Cities," *The Endless City* (London: Phaidon Press, 2008): 342.

72
Richard Sennett, "Civility." *Urban Age*, Bulletin 1, Summer 2005: 1.

10
Carlos Almaraz, *Suburban Nightmare*, 1984.

In the opening line of the 2005 movie *Crash*, police detective Graham comments on a feeling of isolation typical to Los Angeles. "It's the sense of touch. In any real city you walk, you know, you brush past people, people bump into you. In L.A. nobody troubles you. We are always behind all this metal and glass." Artist Carlos Almaraz channeled the desperation of this isolation in his vigorous pastels. *Suburban Nightmare* and *Blue Crash* challenge two of L.A.'s most beloved icons, our private homes and cars. By violently destroying those icons, Almaraz confronts our private isolationist existence, begging for an alternative.

Conversely, "public transit is a socially agreeable kind of mechanical transport; it encourages people to act socially."[71] In transit, one sees, smells, hears, brushes by, sits next to and chats with others, *many* others. Even if you are not paying much attention, your familiarity with your fellow citizens naturally grows in such an environment. This is important.

We Angelenos are not known for easy public congregation; we just don't have much practice at it. Something about the design of this city and how we go about living in it encourages individual freedom and self-expression, yet also encourages intolerance. Whatever happened to civility? Today, it seems to be replaced in L.A. by "road rage," the exact opposite of a culture of reciprocity and respect that constitutes a civil society. The distance and autonomy we have achieved by developing a city based on the car has removed us from the necessity of interaction that naturally occurs in denser, public transit-based cities. In a car-based environment like our "garden city," we don't encounter each other; we don't learn to live with each other, to be civil with each other. We miss one of the truly amazing opportunities great cities can offer: personal and communal enrichment. Richard Sennett wrote, "This should be the promise of urban life: the city's diversity of urban life becoming a source of mutual strength rather than a source of mutual estrangement and civic bitterness."[72]

73
Jennifer Lee, *Civility in the City* (Cambridge, MA: Harvard University Press, 2002): 6.

74
Sennett, "Civility," 2.

What is it that keeps us isolated and makes civility so difficult? L.A.'s culture of hyper-individualism lacks the pedestrian spaces that foster everyday encounters. Jennifer Lee's book *Civility in the City* points out that hundreds of everyday encounters help build civility in even the most struggling communities, such as New York's Harlem and West Philadelphia. [73] Familiarity has no substitute. We, with our differences, need to interact daily. Countless minute public encounters can only happen with a network of well-connected and active plazas, streets and parks. While L.A. has yet to create an effective network of public spaces, it has the potential to cultivate them within its urban structure.

One underutilized feature of this metropolis is our vast network of major boulevards and avenues. Uniquely L.A., these arterials connect cities, districts and a variety of ethnic communities as they meander across valleys, through mountain ranges, over swampy lowlands and rivers. They also tend to run between neighborhoods, acting as the common edges between communities. They function as important urban corridors and connective tissue.

Currently, our boulevards are pieced together, lacking the continuity of space, use and multi-modality that would put them in the company of the great streets of the world. With proper development, they can vastly improve the civility of the city: Los Angeles has often been described as fragmented. But it can be a connected city, and these boulevards can "knit the city together without homogenizing it." [74]

To turn boulevards into world-class urban corridors, the city must offer multi-modal movement opportunities: rail transit, bus, cyclist and pedestrian, as well as automotive. Until recently, most roadways in L.A. have been updated only to accommodate vehicle traffic flow. Even with improvements, the boulevards are congested while putting pedestrians and cyclists at risk. This needs to change.

All major boulevards should accommodate designated bike lanes, not only for the reasons stated above, but also to create an atmosphere of inclusion necessary for a world-class boulevard. The former mayor of Bogota, Enrique Peñalosa, explains, "…it is a powerful symbol, showing that a citizen on a thirty-dollar bicycle is as important as one in a thirty thousand dollar car. A protected bicycle lane along every street is not a cute architectural fixture, but a basic democratic right, unless one believes that only those with access to a car have a right to safe mobility."[75]

Boulevards must be more than commercial corridors. They need to be places where people come together for a variety of reasons, not just to shop or work. Cultural and entertainment facilities, places of worship, youth centers, schools, universities, apartments and hotels all enrich the nature of interaction on boulevards. Most importantly, streets should be the site of public services shared by all, such as post offices, libraries and health services. Placing public services "in the geographic center of a particular community rather than at the edge where that community touches on another of different character," as Sennett states,[76] misses an enormous opportunity to promote everyday interactions between differing communities.

The eminent California historian Kevin Starr said that a city's greatness is measured by the quality of its public spaces. In countless social, economic and environmental ways, everyone in a city benefits from a high-quality pedestrian environment. It is a fundamental component of our democracy. Peñalosa notes that "pavements, bicycle lanes, plazas, parks, promenades, waterfronts and public sports facilities show respect for human dignity and begin at least to compensate for inequality in other realms."[77] How can we expect people to get out of their cars when their cars are much nicer spaces than the sidewalk? Improving the quality of our sidewalks gives them a chance to compete with leather upholstery and surround-sound.

[75] Peñalosa, "Politics, Power, Cities," 313.

[76] Sennett, "Civility," 2.

[77] Peñalosa, "Politics, Power, Cities," 311.

Wilshire Boulevard is a great example of the qualities that Peñalosa cites. Already grand, the extension of the subway will establish this major street as the spinal cord of L.A., linking all of the communities from Downtown to the Pacific Ocean. It crosses three cities and touches upon numerous ethnically diverse communities. The boulevard has high-quality sidewalks, street trees and signage. It has a packed Metro Rapid bus line and the beginnings of a highly anticipated extended subway line. Wilshire is also home to many uses in addition to commercial and residential. Parks, recreation centers, theaters and museums provide recreational and cultural enjoyment. Public and private institutions including universities, libraries, schools, consulates and courthouses provide services, while churches and temples coexist on this special boulevard. As such, it provides an excellent example of how other boulevards in L.A. can draw together communities, even if on a less grand scale. Enhanced development on Wilshire, and increased pedestrian and bike activity, would reinstate Wilshire's potential to become L.A.'s "Main Street."

The Los Angeles River probably provides the best opportunity for open public space in L.A. Its potential to link a multitude of socially diverse communities with open space and recreational venues differentiates it from any public space in Los Angeles, with the possible exception of the beaches. Because of the historical layout of the city, many adjoining land areas are home to obsolete industrial infrastructure, and these too have become regarded as tremendous open space opportunities for the city, such as state parks at Taylor Yard and the Cornfield. The river connects these spaces to many other communities, but these connections have just begun. The riverside's potential for social interaction is immense. Starr observes that the development of open space along the river as well as the reuse of the abandoned Red Car rail lines represents a healing process.

These days we struggle to support initiatives that create the possibility of increased civic space. The effort to create a new "civic plaza" at the steps of City Hall next to the Los Angeles Times building and close to St. Vibiana was thwarted by the decision to build a new police headquarters on the site. It is unfortunate that the police department has replaced a proposed public space where we could have experienced a deeper sense of civility. However, there is still hope for a public space downtown, in the civic park that is part of the Grand Avenue project. Grand Avenue is becoming a cultural centerpiece for L.A., with distinctive architectural gems and the premier orchestra in America.[78] In time, however, this place will be valued not so much for its iconic buildings, but for its public spaces, the boulevard and the civic park, which has long been hidden behind two monolithic county buildings. The connection of the park to the street is crucial. L.A. must encourage the internally focused cultural institutions there to enliven the avenue with programs, displays and other events, demonstrating that they value the street and civic park as extensions of their mission to serve the public and promote a civil society.

These public spaces are crucial at one level because they create a more enriching and impressive city. At another level, as Lee discovered, they are critical settings for the small everyday interactions that foster a culture of reciprocity and respect. We *need* these spaces because they are where "civility and routine are negotiated and maintained each day."[79] This interaction doesn't happen in our cars, and it doesn't happen in our homes; it happens in public spaces that are well-knit into our everyday lives.

[78] Allan Kozinn, "Classical; Continental Shift,"*New York Times*, Arts and Leisure Desk, January 15, 2006.

[79] Lee, *Civility in the City*, 182.

11
Carlos Almaraz, *Blue Crash*, 1984.

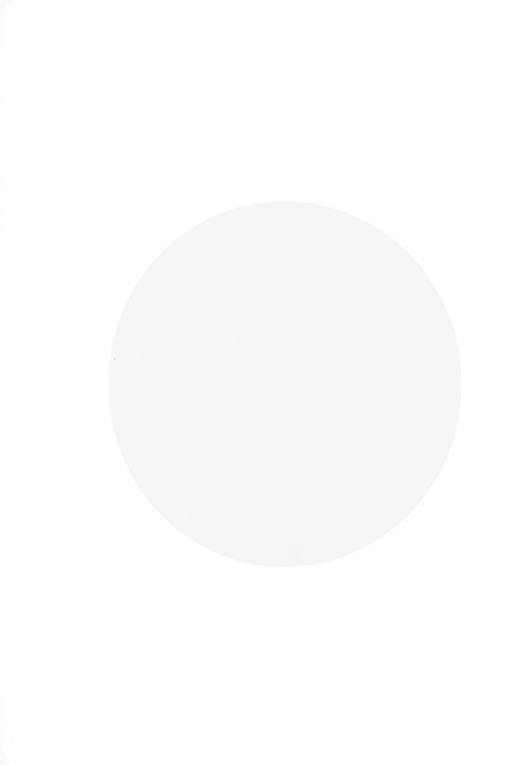

TIME-FORM

Over two thousand years ago, the Tao philosopher Lao Tzu wrote:

Thirty spokes will converge
In the hub of a wheel;
But the use of the cart
Will depend on the part
Of the hub that is void.

With a wall all around
A clay bowl is molded;
But the use of the bowl
Will depend on the part
Of the bowl that is void.

Cut out windows and doors
In the house as you build;
But the use of the house
Will depend on the space
In the walls that is void.

So advantage is had
From whatever is there;
But usefulness rises
From whatever is not. [80]

[80]
Lao Tzu poem "San-shih fu" or "Thirty Spokes," translated by Raymond B. Blakney and published in *The Way of Life: Lao Tzu* (New York: Penguin Putnam Inc., New American Library, 2001): 63.

"But usefulness rises from whatever is not" refers to the space created by form, the yin to the yang. Form and space are inseparable and equally important, yet architects traditionally focus on building form, to the detriment of the spaces that the building or buildings create. In design magazines and architecture schools around the world, there is an obsession with dramatic shapes and how they are made, neglecting the spaces those shapes make and how they function.

This is especially true in Los Angeles. It has been too easy for architects to forget about designing the relationship between buildings, resulting in a dearth of intentional and functional urban space. This alienation of space and form is expressed by contemporary artists such as Wayne Thiebaud, who depicted detached roadways swirling around isolated buildings. To counter this trend, as Lao Tzu suggests in his poem, architects need to consider both; space is as much a design product as the materials and geometries that define it.

There is a third part of this relationship that is crucial for designers to understand: time. The wisdom of the ancient Chinese text *I Ching* helps us to clearly see the dynamic interplay of opposites such as form and space in all environments. Form and space are not static, but are an evolution of events with only one certainty: that change is inevitable. This dynamic interplay of opposites is explored vividly in artist Bill Viola's video work *Memoria*. During a 2003 forum at the J. Paul Getty Museum, Viola explained how he established a contextual field of fractal-like shapes by using a veil in darkness through which the camera strains to find "traces of light." In fact, he describes it as "a thick, grainy texture that suggests the violence and perpetual creativity of recombinant matter, atoms and molecules forming and reforming, a haze of infinite possibility, an aura or spiritual eminence, the fabric of the universe."[81] Slowly, a face emerges and recedes through this murky field. It is this emergence of form as pattern within its context that Viola calls "time-form." This relationship is no less embodied by cities, which have an urban time-form. Like the imagery emerging and dissolving in Viola's murky field, cities have an ever-changing contextual field of which buildings and spaces are a part.[82]

Los Angeles' contextual field is a distinct urban fabric expressed on a variety of levels: local neighborhood centers, more pedestrian in scale with mixed use and in some cases higher densities; spread-out multiple communities like the "Westside," "Downtown," the "Harbor Area" and

81
Bill Viola quoted in *Bill Viola: The Passions*, by John Walsh (editor), Kira Perov (photographer), and Peter Sellars (contributor), (Los Angeles: Getty Publications, 2003): 173.

82
This ever-changing contextual field is what Richard Weinstein calls the "mulch" of the city, as explored in "Understanding Bigness."

12

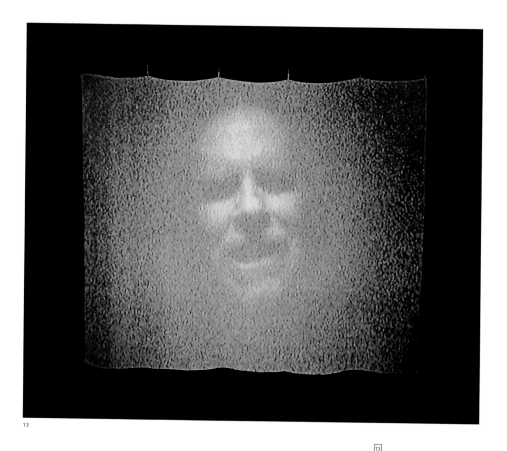

13

83
Jacobs, *Death and Life*,
443-444.

"Boyle Heights"; or at a regional scale, building upon the "super grid" of city streets and freeways. If one has not yet been to an area of the city one can fill in the blank because of the spatial order and clarity of the overall system. As Los Angeles evolves and densifies over time, the interrelationship of buildings to urban space will become tighter and more defined. Sprawl has allowed us to ignore urban space; densification allows us the opportunity to create new urban space.

As architects, we need to understand the evolution of form and space in the city as a process, not as a fixed sculptural condition. The construction of a building is not the beginning or the end of the story, but just one act in an ever-changing urban landscape. Even though designers think of their creations as permanent, in reality—due to the inevitability of change—they are transformed with different uses over time. The longest lasting buildings and neighborhoods typically are the most adaptable.

Landscape architects understand their work as a dynamic process involving plants, seasons and weather. This has evolved into the Landscape Urbanism movement we see today. Architects and planners have mostly ignored such processes, focused on the frozen image, despite the fact that their materials and conditions are likewise dynamic, and their human clients, arguably the most creative creatures on earth, continually act upon their environments. "Human beings are, of course, a part of nature, as much so as grizzly bears or bees or whales or sorghum cane. The cities of human beings are as natural, being a product of one form of nature, as are the colonies of prairie dogs or the beds of oysters." [83]

In the urban habitat, public space holds the life-blood of the city: street space, plaza and park space, the passages and courts between buildings. People enjoy life within these spaces; they re-create the city continually through personal and communal events within them. To neglect the dynamism of urban space is to neglect the life of the city. The vitality, civility, and community of cities depend upon what urbanist

Richard Sennett calls "democratic space," an "unregulated life on the ground plane,"[84] and what art critic Nicolas Bourriaud calls "arenas of exchange."[85]

Sennett challenges designers to create and pay special attention to urban elements: incomplete form and public spaces called "passage territories." Sennett argues that these elements, implemented effectively, can "abet social relationships that endure through being given the opportunity to evolve and mutate."[86] When they are porous and incomplete they provide opportunities for democratic engagement. Incomplete forms refer to built structures that invite growth of other structures around it, with the "buildings acquiring specific urban value through their relationship to one another; in time they become incomplete forms when considered by themselves."[87] Together, these forms and spaces facilitate one of the magical qualities of great cities, that over time, the whole is increasingly more valuable and interesting than the sum of its parts.

[84] Sennett, "The Open City," The Endless City (London: Phaidon Press, 2008): 290.

[85] Nicolas Bourriaud, *Relational Aesthetics* (Paris: Les Presses Du Reel, 1998): 4th paragraph under subheading "Artwork as social interstice."

[86] Sennett, "The Open City": 293.

[87] ibid

TRASH

The world is too much with us; late and soon,
Getting and spending, we lay waste our powers;
Little we see in Nature that is ours;
We have given our hearts away, a sordid boon!

William Wordsworth

As the SUV neared the intersection, a half-full two-liter plastic Coke bottle flew out into the street. The driver rushed to make the signal, passed through the intersection and roared down Sunset Boulevard, the environment now burdened with one more piece of trash. As I watched this unfold from my bike, I was reminded of our collective irresponsibility toward our environment. Our environmental situation is the result of a cultural problem.

What is culture? While the topic has generated a range of definitions over the centuries, most agree that "culture" denotes a set of shared attitudes, values and practices that characterize a group. Culture is learned and transmitted through signs, symbols and language. These shape our society and establish norms of behavior that reinforce our attitudes toward our community and nation, our use of natural resources and our relationship to the earth. The consequences of everyday actions in a culture that is not environmentally sensitive about consumption and waste management are devastating. To the contrary, if a culture respects the environment, the sum of everyday actions can make a substantial positive impact on the environment.

While many well-intentioned groups in the United States are fighting to curb environmental degradation through governmental means, legislating behavior is difficult when an electorate is predisposed to a lifestyle based on excessive consumption. In fact, our culture rewards those who can consume the most with enhanced social status, communicating that "size does matter." Disregard for the environment is so pervasive that more often than not we do not even recognize it.

Ironically, most of us believe in environmental sustainability—we agree that it's the right thing to do. But while holding this view intellectually, sadly, too many of us continue to "shop till we drop" and feel "whoever dies with the most toys wins." In *The Social Contract*, Jean-Jacques Rousseau concludes that the social pact of a society is based upon the voluntary agreement of its members to act together for the benefit of that society. In so doing, each member benefits from being part of the society but also agrees to surrender "his natural [i.e., unlimited] liberty and the absolute right to anything that tempts him and that he can take."[88] Are we so driven to consume that we are unable to see the need for restraint? If our "social contract" is so heavily influenced by consumption as to pillage our natural resources and pollute the landscape, what good is the contract?

In 1948, naturalist Aldo Leopold addressed this fundamental contradiction between American culture and a proper respect for nature. An internationally recognized scientist, he spent his career with the National Forest Service. Leopold recognized that our culture seldom values maintaining the natural environment over consuming natural resources for lifestyle needs. He was concerned that although man is inevitably a part of nature, he has detached himself, resulting in an essential conflict: "man the conqueror versus man the biotic citizen."[89] Leopold's land ethic attempts to establish conditions for a new respect for nature.

To realize how far we are from Leopold's land ethic, it is helpful to examine other cultural examples. I have had this opportunity on two separate occasions: one, working with American Indians in Oklahoma, and the other on a recent trip to The Kingdom of Bhutan.

Nearly fifteen years ago, we received a telephone inquiry from Ron Rosenthal, secretary of commerce for the state of Oklahoma, about our interest in designing a cultural center and museum for the thirty-nine federally recognized American Indian tribes of the state. The project

88
Jean-Jacques Rousseau, *The Social Contract, Or Principles of Political Right* (New York: Penguin Classics, Modern Reprint Edition, 1968): 65.

89
Aldo Leopold, *Sand County Almanac* (New York: Ballantine Books, 1986): 260.

was to commemorate the Oklahoma Indians, who had been forcibly relocated to Oklahoma following the passage of the Congressional Act of 1830, along the "Trail of Tears." What began as a straightforward site-selection study became a profound architectural project. The project is currently in construction and will most likely take another four years to complete. Although an unusually long design process for a project of its scale, the time has been necessary to develop a subtler understanding of the Oklahoma Indians.

The 280-acre site—generously given to the Native American Cultural and Educational Authority by the City of Oklahoma City—is within the area defined as Oil Drilling Site #1, essentially the first oil discovery in the state. Early photography documents massive oil extraction activities, which led to heavy contamination. As the site was originally Indian Territory, the tribes were delighted to regain what had originally been theirs. The next step was to restore the site to its pristine state, cleaning up the salt waste deposits left from the oil drilling, restoring wetlands along the Oklahoma River, and replanting native grasses and vegetation. The underlying belief is that man originates from the earth and eventually ascends to the heavens. To the Indians, our Cultural Center building had to *engage* the earth because earth and building are inseparable.

Emile Durkheim's studies of totemic religion in *The Elementary Forms of Religious Life* found that all societies have a way of distinguishing what is considered sacred from the *profane*, or mundane. What a society considers sacred, he observed, instigates protective actions from its members. The American Indians' way of life and everyday actions reflect the view that the earth and its inhabitants are sacred. Colors, numbers, materials—each has meaning. For American Indians, life is circular, meaning that in the course of one's life one can expect to come upon a circumstance in one form or another that had previously occurred.

The four elements of earth, wind, water and fire are fundamental. Fire is sacred; each tribe has unique ceremonies involving fire, to represent its power and significance for life. The sun's orientation is a seasonal clock, helping to determine the time to plant and harvest, as the sunrise is a determinant of the orientation of dwellings. Most importantly, the Indians have a respect for the earth; it is "Mother Earth." Earth is spiritual and sacred.

It was for this reason that the American Indians did not understand the concept of *trading* earth as if it were a commodity. Because the Indians' respect for the earth was and is fundamental to their way of life, degrading it in any way would be unthinkable. This is best expressed by the Great Law of Peace, the oral constitution of the Iroquois people dating from the eleventh century, which states that man should plan and conserve for the coming seven generations. As the Iroquois declare: "For centuries we have known that each individual's action creates conditions and situations that affect the world. For centuries we have been careful to avoid any action unless it carried a long-range prospect of promoting harmony and peace in the world."[90] Here lies the fundamental difference between the two approaches to life. In the minds of the Western European settlers, who did not regard the natural environment as sacred, land was very much a commodity to be traded. This attitude seems to have led to the contemporary ethic of "let's consume as much as possible, right now." The Iroquois reaction to this disregard was a strong warning expressed to the United Nations in Geneva, in 1977: "Today the species of Man is facing a question of the very survival of the species. The way of life known as Western Civilization is on a death path [for] which their own culture has no viable answers. When faced with the reality of their own destructiveness, they can only go forward into areas of more efficient destruction."[91]

I observed an ethic similar to that of the American Indians while traveling in Bhutan in 2009. The country is located in the Himalaya Mountains

[90] Representatives of the Iroquois Confederacy, "A Basic Call to Consciousness: The Hau de no sau nee Address to the Western World," Mohawk Nation: *Akwesasne Notes*, 1978: Part 3. (http://www.ratical.com/many_worlds/6Nations/6nations3.html#part3).

[91] Representatives of the Iroquois Confederacy, Part 1a. (http://www.ratical.com/many_worlds/6Nations/6nations1.html#part1a).

bordering Nepal to the west, India to the south and east, and Tibet and China to the north. Bhutan is so remote that it has only been reasonably accessible to westerners in the twentieth century. Although connected for centuries by a maze of footpaths, its first cross-kingdom paved road was not constructed until the 1960s, and its only airport was not built until 1974.

For the last one hundred years the kingdom has been ruled by the Wangchuck royal family. In the interest of allowing the citizens greater freedom, in 2007 the king initiated a new democratic form of government, which many citizens have accepted only with reservations. Although Drukpa Buddhist culture has helped to unify the country with a common ethic about the environment, the country has several geographical divides because of its topography. Today, three major ethnic groups exist, making homogenous cultural identity difficult; yet each shares a deep-felt respect for the environment. Western influence has been limited, and even today the population is mostly farm-based and dispersed throughout the countryside. The intimate relationship between the population and the natural setting is fundamental. Unlike many of its neighboring countries, the countryside is pristine. Bhutan is one of the planet's great centers of biodiversity. Seventy-two percent of the geographic area remains natural forest; of this, 36 percent is devoted to parks and wildlife corridors. The country's constitution mandates that 60 percent of the country should remain natural, forever. When one visits the country it is apparent that the population has exercised enormous restraint in order to conserve nature.

For the Bhutanese, everything that lives is to be respected. This is largely the result of a belief in reincarnation. Land is spiritual and land gods called "nagas" exist everywhere. We were told that no one goes to high altitudes on the snow-lined peaks because the spirits forbid it, although this is most likely due to the dangerous conditions at great altitudes. We were told another story about a guide who took stones from one side of a river to the other side. The guide fell ill until his cousin returned to the river and relocated the stones to their original positions. The guide immediately recovered from his illness.

The construction of Bhutanese farmhouses perhaps best illustrates the culture's sensitivity to the natural environment. When a family decides to build a new house, a site is selected with the help of a Buddhist monk and the local builder-architect. Led by the monk, the family and construction team then go into the nearby forest to select the appropriate trees for construction. Care is given to select trees whose felling would least disturb the forest, yet are appropriate for building a strong dwelling. The building site is carefully cleared and the foundation is set with minimum cut and fill of soil. As the earthen walls go up, neighborhood women join in to pack the rammed earth walls. They sing traditional songs in the process. This is reminiscent of the "barn-raising" custom in Midwestern communities from earlier times. As windows and doorframes are set into place, the monk returns to bless the openings. A niche is built into the exterior wall of the home as a shrine to the nagas. There, on a regular basis, a prayer is given to express appreciation for the home and its natural setting. Building is a religious act.

The importance of the environment is embedded in Bhutanese culture. Although laws in Bhutan prohibit environmental degradation, the everyday actions of its people reflect this ethic far more powerfully. It illustrates a deep belief that man is connected to the natural environment, and that with care and respect, nature's complex relationships can be maintained. Whether or not this unique country can serve as a model for us is questionable. Its land ethic has taken centuries to develop and the Western world must deal with its own complex factors.

We need to consider how to shift our cultural attitudes of exaggerated consumption and corresponding disrespect for the natural environment

92
Leopold, *Sand County Almanac*, 261.

toward a new land ethic. Culture is learned. Each younger generation learns from the elder, through the home, formal education, the media and through community example.

Formal Education in the Classroom: Aldo Leopold observed that "...perhaps the most serious obstacle impeding the evolution of a land ethic is the fact that our educational and economic system is headed away from, rather than towards, an intense consciousness of land."[92] Even though our educational systems are being challenged by increased class size, under-compensated teachers and low test scores, education is essential to understanding the environment. From primary school to the university, education provides the underpinning of a culture that respects the environment. This includes all of our individual everyday acts that, in total, could improve our world.

Media: The media can be a powerful tool in educating the population about environmental issues. Instead of trying to influence us to eat unhealthy hamburgers and to buy cars shown speeding across desert flats, television programming could be telling us about ways to conserve the earth's resources, to use renewable energy and to treat our environment in other sustainable ways.

Community Example: How wonderful it would be if younger generations could learn a culture of service from today's society. Service-focused programs could not only benefit our communities, but also positively shape the cultural values of those who participate. In 1961, President Kennedy established the Peace Corps. One could enlist for two years and travel to remote locations throughout the world to help communities and peoples in need. It has always been closely aligned to an emerging appreciation and respect for nature. The Peace Corps has inspired the creation of many similar programs including AmeriCorps, Senior Corps, Green Corps and Teach for America, among others. With more of us taking advantage of national service opportunities like this, our society and its land ethic will most certainly improve.

There are examples of progressive achievements that provide an opportunity for a degree of optimism. Communities in the Pacific Northwest, from the San Francisco Bay Area up to Vancouver, British Columbia, exhibit a high degree of appreciation for the outdoors. In these communities, cultural values weigh heavily in favor of environmental matters, and the everyday actions of their citizens reflect this.

There is still much to be done to upgrade our cultural norms. We need to change our culture, our way of *being* in the world. This requires an examination of our attitudes, values, goals and everyday actions; it translates into what we do in our communities, what is taught in our schools and what is conveyed in the media. If we change, we influence others to change, and our culture changes.

THE INFORMATION AGE IS USHERING IN A NEW URBAN FORM, THE INFORMATIONAL CITY. [93]

Manuel Castells

93
Manuel Castells, *The Rise of the Network Society* (Malden, MA: Blackwell Publishers, 1996): 429.

As a result of the expanding knowledge economy, new models for urbanization are emerging with the increased speed and affordability of worldwide electronic communication. New markets and economies have been created and repositioned by the Internet. "Knowledge industries" are a prime force in the global economy. Cities become more important as crossroads for information flow. They are the nodes in a world network where transactions, innovations and markets occur. The cities that will have the most influence, power and success will depend upon how competitively they adapt to this economy.

The importance of competing in this arena became all too apparent during a recent visit to China. There is nowhere better to witness the physical development of the "knowledge city." Its job formation is vigorous. The government has embarked on major infrastructure building programs. It is as if the Maoist period between 1949 and 1989 was a brief pause for a culture that is increasingly comfortable navigating the global economy.

The Chinese assume that education is key to improving the prosperity of their nation, and they are building what they call "University Cities" to accomplish this. Four or five existing universities form a consortium and develop a University City, usually located within or near an existing city.

The proposed student population ranges up to as many as one hundred thousand students. Mao Zedong tried to send the teachers into the rural farm areas, citing that both teacher and farmer could learn from each other. Today's program is just the opposite. Rural people are allowed to migrate to urban areas in order to better themselves with new education and employment. This immigration is understandable, as farm wages are often less than $1000 a year, while a new job in Shanghai can bring a salary of $10,000 or more.

Returning to the United States, one sees the opposite. With the 2008 recession, declining employment and the dismantling of our job base, most U.S. employees are experiencing the devolution of their knowledge society. While our major cities hold special positions in the world economy, these positions are threatened by ambitious cities around the world. Cities like the fifteen in China that are expected to reach populations of 25 million each within the next fifteen years are quickly rising to meet the demands of the knowledge economy. [94]

Like New York City and Chicago, Los Angeles is considered one of the world's established global cities. [95] Los Angeles has many advantages in the current economy. It has a wealth of knowledge-based industries. Last year, *Foreign Policy* reported that L.A.'s film and media industry earned nearly thirty billion dollars in box-office revenue, which amounts to Kenya's entire entire Gross Domestic Product (GDP). [96] For decades it was the center of the world's largest high-technology defense complex. [97] Los Angeles has a wealth of distinguished institutions of higher education. In 2007, L.A. ranked second in the world only to New York City in the number of universities, [98] colleges, institutes and graduate universities.

Cities with young populations like Los Angeles tend to have advantages over cities with large older populations since the young adjust quickly to the evolving needs of the knowledge workforce. "Rust belt" cities are losing ground because of the continuing decline of manufacturing

[94] Parag Khanna, "Beyond City Limits: The age of nations is over. The new urban age has begun," *Foreign Policy*, September/October 2010: 18th paragraph.

[95] A.T. Kearny, the Chicago Council on Foreign Affairs and *Foreign Policy, The Global Cities Index 2010*, Foreign Policy, August 2010.

[96] Brian Fung and Jared Mondschein, "Metropolis Now: Images of the World's Top Global Cities," *Foreign Policy*, August 16, 2010: "7. Los Angeles."

[97] Castells, Network Society, 422.

[98] MasterCard Worldwide, 2007.

99
MasterCard
Worldwide,2008.

100
Peter F. Drucker, "Will the
Corporation Survive?" *The
Economist*, November 1,
2001: 3rd paragraph under
subheading "Everything in
its place."

101
Peñalosa, "Politics, Power,
Cities," 319.

102
Margaret O'Mara, "Don't
Try This at Home: You can't
build a new Silicon Valley
just anywhere," *Foreign
Policy*, September/October
2010: 1st paragraph under
subheading "3. Don't forget
that location matters."

jobs and the flight of young people to cities with growing knowledge-based jobs. Los Angeles also boasts a large entrepreneurial immigrant population, a strong small business environment, and exceptional cultural and recreational offerings.

Despite these advantages, Los Angeles is in danger of losing ground to other world cities as a place for knowledge workers. In 2007, Los Angeles ranked as the tenth best center for business in the world, which is admirable given major cities in Europe and Asia. Yet by 2008 the city's ranking had slipped to seventeenth.[99] Three problem areas stand out as major handicaps for Los Angeles in the global economy: pre-university education, traffic congestion and environmental quality.

If L.A. has so many advantages, why do these three problem areas matter? In the knowledge economy, a city's quality of life matters tremendously. For L.A. to compete globally, it must continue to attract, retain and develop knowledge workers. The means of production today is knowledge, which, as economist Peter Drucker points out, "...is owned by knowledge workers and is highly portable."[100] It was formerly the employer that L.A. worked hard to attract. Today, businesses will locate wherever there is an abundance of qualified knowledge workers. Qualified knowledge workers are highly mobile, choosing to live where they can have the best life. As the former mayor of Bogotá, Enrique Peñalosa, points out, "now it is necessary to create environments to which wealth-creating people are attracted... More important than tax rates or port infrastructure, urban quality of life can be the most valued competitive factor in the new economy."[101] Margaret O'Mara, who studied the origins of the knowledge-economy mecca Silicon Valley, explained, Silicon Valley prospered because it had the qualities that attracted people who had the education, economic resources and social advantages to live anywhere they chose."[102]

Because the fastest growing-job categories in the U.S. are in knowledge-based technology and technology-related industries, all young people will require a quality education to be able to enter the workforce. Cities that have high-achieving K-12 schools, in addition to excellent higher education campuses, are a premium for knowledge workers because they want their children to have access to the finest education.

It is clear that public education is crucial to a city's competitiveness; however, public education is a problem in Los Angeles. The city may be home to excellent institutions of higher learning, but many of our young people do not complete their high school education. Recent articles in the *Los Angeles Times* have underscored the complexity of the crisis in our schools. Parents, administrators, teachers and students must find a shared vision of how to bring schools into this new economy. Los Angeles' broken school system is failing its large and diverse population of young people. It is clear that whoever "out-educates us today is going to out-compete us tomorrow."[103]

Another barrier to competing in the knowledge economy is the traffic congestion and poor environmental air quality associated with L.A.'s dependence on the automobile. Los Angeles is considered to be one of the most automobile-congested cities in the United States. We have a difficult time believing that we need multi-modal mobility, despite ever-increasing complaints about travel time to work, congestion at all hours on freeways, bad air quality, and the increasing distance to affordable housing and good schools. Although voters recently passed bond issues for new transit lines, the timing of funding has made it difficult to construct them within a reasonable life span. This is unacceptable and threatens to alter the city's quality of life.

Clearly, in the knowledge city, speed of movement is of the utmost importance. We must develop our information infrastructure to become as "frictionless" and "smart" as possible. Major cities around the

[103]
Thomas L. Friedman quoting President Barack Obama in "Teaching for America." *New York Times*, November 20, 2010: 1st paragraph.

104
Khanna, *Beyond City Limits,*
11th paragraph.

world are making great strides in creating highly mobile and efficient environments, in the hopes of drawing knowledge workers away from places like Los Angeles.[104]

Poor environmental quality does not just mean air and water quality, but also the quality of urban places that promote social encounters. Years ago the common belief was that, with the Internet, cities would become even more decentralized, i.e., people could move beyond the suburbs to areas unconstrained by urban boundaries. It was commonly said that you could live on your ranch in Montana and conduct business as usual from your home. This has occurred, but not to the degree expected. The surprise was that increased communications vastly increase the need for face-to-face interaction. L.A. has an adequate network of indoor meeting places, but it currently lacks outdoor public spaces and walkable environments that promote interaction at a broader level of society.

Los Angeles is a world-class city, and a trendsetter for the early knowledge economy that emerged in the twentieth century. Today, we must strive to compete internationally. We need to re-imagine Los Angeles as a more public and inclusive metropolis to fulfill its potential as a world leader in the knowledge economy.

CREATIVE ISLAND

105

Carey McWilliams, *Southern California: An Island on the Land*, (Layton, UT: Gibbs Smith, 1973): 369.

Southern California is a "great tribal burial ground for antique customs," an environment conducive to imaginative thinking. "Here on the Western shore, a society had been formed that was 'more mobile and unstable, less governed by fixed beliefs and principles'... No notion is more deeply seated, no idea has echoed more persistently throughout the years than the theory that a new and vital culture would some day be born in California."[105] With a forgiving Mediterranean climate, lack of formal urban constraints and inherent diversity, this region gave birth to one of the most unique and creative cities in the world: Los Angeles.

Despite the Mediterranean analogy, architects from Greene and Greene, Irving Gill and Richard Neutra to Thom Mayne, Frank Gehry, Ray Kappe and Eric Owen Moss rejected traditional styles, and instead experimented boldly with unique architectural form and new concepts of urban living. Following World War II, John Entenza and the Case Study Houses involving architects such as Pierre Koenig, Charles and Rae Eames and Craig Ellwood began to reach the world through *Arts and Architecture* magazine, asserting the importance of the Southland as a setting for innovative and imaginative design.

The unique setting of this city seems to spark and nourish the creative spirit of individual artists, designers and entrepreneurs. While participating in a symposium on public space at UCLA in 1999, I was struck by how fellow speaker David Hockney spoke about the spatial quality of the city. He told of returning to Los Angeles from London, arriving at his hillside residence and setting out at sunset in a convertible, driving along Mulholland toward Malibu. He spoke of the enormous freedom he felt, and how dramatically the spatial quality of the city affected his work. Other artists were similarly affected, particularly Ron Davis, Ed Ruscha, Larry Bell, Peter Alexander and Ed Moses in the 1960s and 1970s.

Rick Smith, president of CBS Records in the 1970s, was surprised by the creativity and tenacity of individual musicians in Los Angeles. In New York, agents professionally mediated the promotion of their artists to Smith, whereas, during his visits to L.A., he was continually approached at his Beverly Hills Hotel suite by the artists themselves, who felt free to promote their own work at any opportunity.

Los Angeles has weathered explosive growth, decay, the triumph of the 1984 Olympics and disasters such as earthquakes and riots. Space and ethnicity have changed dramatically in Los Angeles over the past several decades. We develop less in suburban locations and are adaptively reusing and infilling inner city areas, increasing density to that of more traditional cities. However, problems of schooling, transportation and air pollution remain.

I wonder if the Los Angeles environment continues to evoke such creative spirits. What better way to address these questions than to compare the Los Angeles American Institute of Architects awards of 1975 and 2005, two snapshots of L.A.'s architectural history.

In the 1975 awards, juried by Esther McCoy, Richard Meier, Gunnar Birkerts and Romaldo Giurgola, twenty awards were given; in 2005, there were nineteen. Although L.A. has long been identified with suburbs of single family homes, neither awards program was dominated by residential architecture. In 1975, Frank Gehry and Cesar Pelli received three awards each; other winners included Anthony Lumsden at DMJM, AC Martin, Quincy Jones, Ray Kappe and Lomax Mills. Many of the large, commercial structures have not weathered the test of time and would not be recognized in today's program. One project that was lauded for having "great simplicity and dignity" would likely be seen today as banal modernism. Gehry's projects began to portend his future; his design for Ron Davis' studio/residence acknowledges less an idea about a stand-alone building and more about the relationships between "live" and "work," as well as an emerging

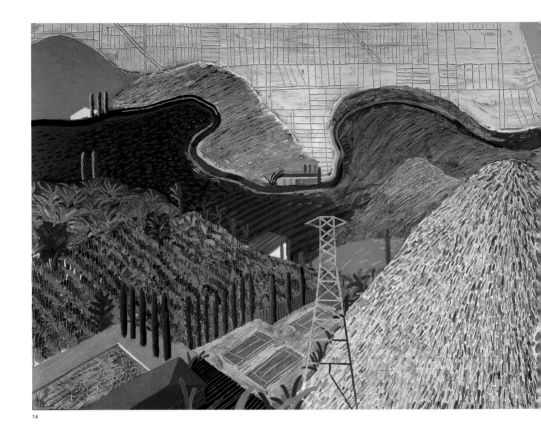

14

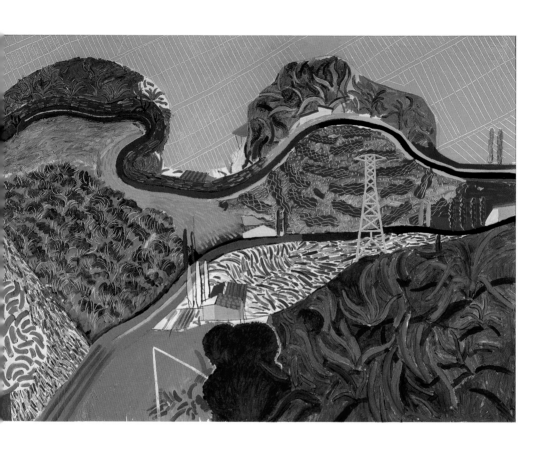

relationship between architect and artist. In 1975, architecture projects were modernist in vernacular, meant to be viewed only as individual objects without consideration of their urban contexts. Noticeably absent in the 1975 program were urban design projects. It was as if influence from urban design work being done at the time in New York City and elsewhere had not yet reached the West Coast.

In 2005, projects were significantly more complex, with greater project diversity and use of context and environment as generators of formal ideas. This was an optimistic trend for those of us who would like to see greater acknowledgement of urban design in the program. Several of the 2005 awards recognize projects that are creatively opportunistic and contextual—perhaps reflecting an emerging urbanism. The awards were given to a broad range of firms, rather than being dominated by a few individuals as in 1975. Only RoTo Architects and Eric Owen Moss received second awards. The diversity of projects ranges from Doug Suisman's bold Arc urban design plan for Palestine to an ethereal art installation at the Venice Biennale by Predock Frane. The stand-alone corporate headquarters of 1975 had been replaced by institutional projects such as Thom Mayne's California Department of Transportation (Caltrans) regional headquarters and mixed-use projects like Moss' Conjunctive Points Theater Complex—both incredibly imaginative and individually expressive in response to challenging contexts. The Children's Museum, by agps architecture, was a new interpretation of interactive and green environments. Pugh + Scarpa's Solar Umbrella was a beautifully executed building that took the Case Studies to the next step. Creative multi-family urban infill was not a priority in 1975, but in 2005 two projects, by Montalba Architects and Osborn Architects embodied positive assumptions about incremental development while exploiting new zoning opportunities. Koning Eizenberg's adaptive reuse at the Standard Hotel and Clive Wilkinson Architects' interiors for Mother Advertising London were both inconceivable projects in 1975—let alone an attention to sustainable building systems.

The 2005 projects are representative of a more mature culture, yet these interesting and diverse schemes continue the Southland tradition as a hotbed of architectural creativity and innovation. Given all the changes L.A. has undergone in recent decades, what qualities remain that keep this creativity alive? One quality is a flexible landscape. Peter Alexander captures this in his painting, *Van Nuys*, which illustrates Los Angeles' vast grid of streets.

The city has long been criticized by those in more traditional cities for this endless urban fabric and for lacking a "proper," i.e., traditional, downtown. In 1948, Carey McWilliams wrote, "…Southern California constitutes a single metropolitan district which should be characterized as *rurban*: neither city nor country but everywhere a mixture of both. Just as Southern California is the least rural of all the regions in America, so, paradoxically, Los Angeles is the least citified of all regions in America." [106] He continues this point by quoting geographer J. Russell Smith who said, "Nowhere in the United States is it more difficult to draw a line between city life, suburban life, and country life." [107] L.A.'s landscape still defies all categorization—what else is suburban, urban, rural and wild all mixed together in a frequently tossed big salad? This is why it is possible to live a quiet country life on the edge of downtown, and how a suburb in Hollywood could be denser than most central cities in the nation. Wild bobcats and coyotes are a continual threat to urban pets, and wildfires covering hundreds of acres can occur in the middle of the city. [108]

David Hockney has characterized Los Angeles as a perfect setting for independent, creative thinking; individual actions, entrepreneurship and experimentation thrive. Painters, artists and designers do well here, as do small businesses. Mayor Villaraigosa recently announced that L.A. is home to more small businesses than any other city in the country, and emphasized this with the startling statistic that 70 percent of Angelenos are employed by small businesses.

[106] McWilliams, *Southern California*, 12, italics inserted.

[107] J. Russell Smith quoted by McWilliams, *Southern California*, 13.

[108] These remarkably dynamic conditions were illustrated at the Natural History Museum of Los Angeles County in its 2004 exhibit: LA: light/motion/dreams.

109
David Malmuth and Jack Skelley, "The Capital of Creativity: Ethnic-focused development and residential innovation highlight Southern California's economic dynamism," *Urban Land*, September 2005: 86.

110
Esa-Pekka Salonen quoted by Kozinn in "Classical; Continental Shift," 17th paragraph.

Peter Alexander, *Van Nuys*, 1987. Oil on canvas, 60" x 66".

The city offers an open invitation. Ed Ruscha talks about driving Route 66 from Oklahoma City to L.A. after high school to settle in this "land of opportunity." Today, the city is exceptional in its diversity, making it "a rich gumbo of multicultural empowerment."[109] Los Angeles is one of the most racially diverse cities in the U.S., if not the world; almost 40 percent of its residents are foreign-born. While not always living in perfect harmony, these many groups of varied ethnicities and backgrounds undoubtedly influence each other.

Designers and artists who live or visit L.A. are deeply affected by this astounding collection of cultures. Esa-Pekka Salonen, who conducted the L.A. Philharmonic between 1992 and 2009, describes, "It was a very complicated process for me. I come from Finland, which is the most homogenous society in Europe. There is almost no diversity. And then I land here, and whatever you might call this society, homogenous is not the word. And I eventually realized that my Eurocentric, rather rigid Northern European ideas were not necessarily valid in a culture that has this many layers and this degree of diversity."[110]

L.A.'s messy, aesthetically challenged multi-flavored everyday urbanism is an ideal arena for those who think "outside the box." It provides a collection of environments that challenge you, sometimes merely through their strange juxtaposition. L.A. is alive with struggle—the struggle of millions of people working simultaneously for a better life, sometimes through conflicting means. Not everything is worked out neatly in this agglomeration. Architects and urban designers often feel they need to provide society with perfect utopian places, where every concern is under control. This leads to fantasyland planning, creating places where the pressing realities of today's world are far away, and is a delusionary disservice. If cities exist to foster human growth, they must be places where people can act creatively, places where diverse cultures interact. The exciting promise of the city is that despite its struggles, Los Angeles, as a creative island, is alive and well.

15

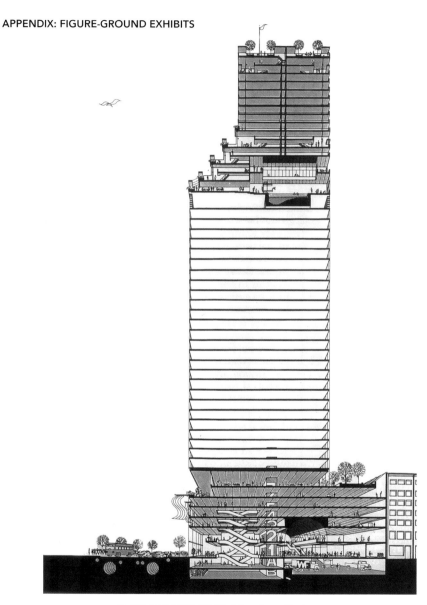

1a. Fifth Avenue Mixed-Use Prototype. Image Courtesy
Jonathan Barnett, *Urban Design as Public Policy. Practical
Methods for Improving Cities* (New York: Architectural
Record Books, 1974) 54

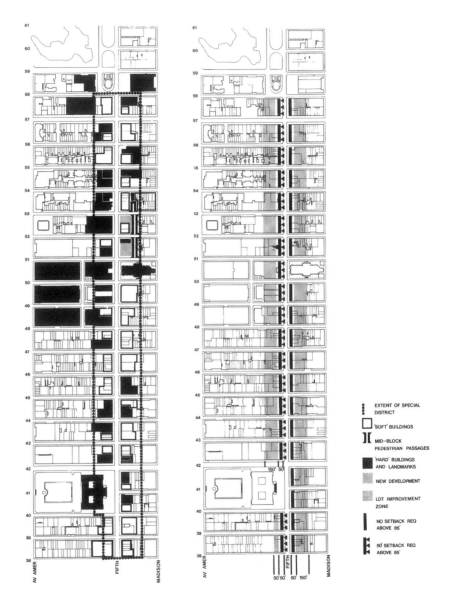

1b. Fifth Avenue Special Purpose Zoning District. Image
Courtesy Jonathan Barnett, *Urban Design as Public
Policy. Practical Methods for Improving Cities* (New York:
Architectural Record Books, 1974) 53

2a. Los Angeles Existing Open Space

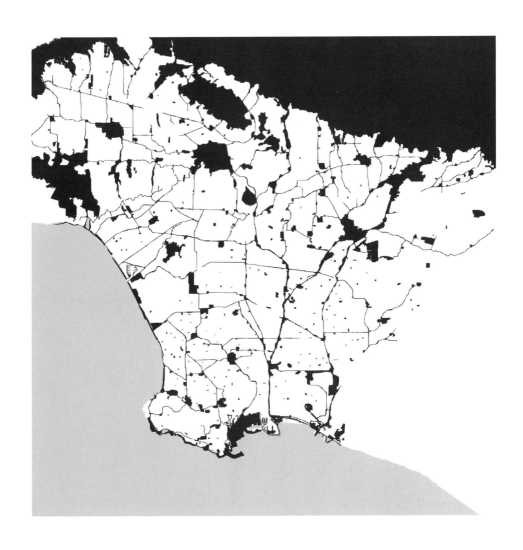

2b. With Greenways

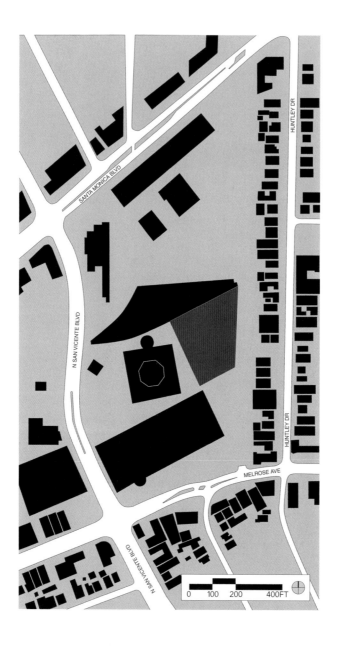

3. Pacific Design Center

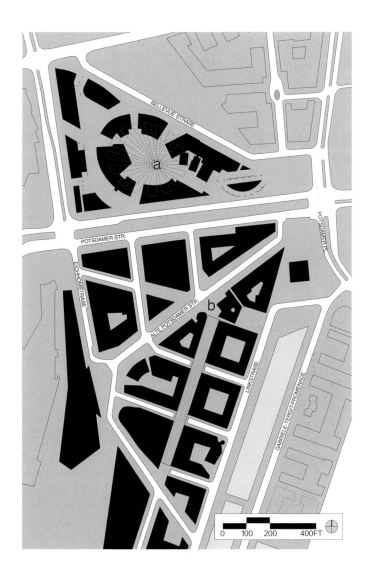

4. Potsdamer Platz
a. Sony Center by Helmut Jahn
b. Daimler AG Project involved multiple architects for
independent projects

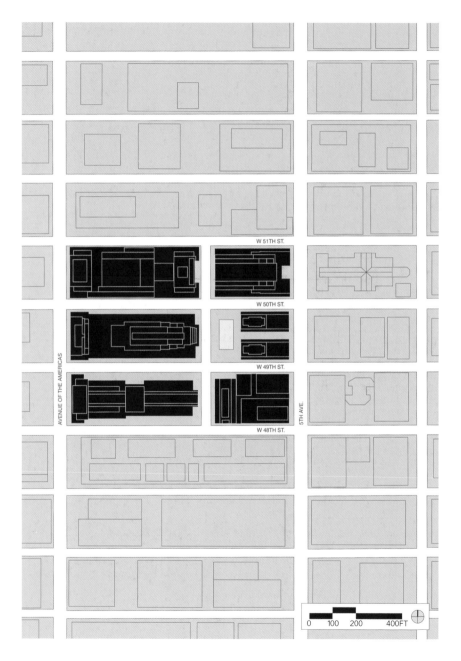

5. Rockefeller Center

6. China Central Television (CCTV) Headquarters

7a. Malmö Bo01 (As Built)

7b. Malmö Bo01 (Enlargement-Planned)
The overall complex was designed by twenty-two separate
architects; all buildings labeled No.6, for example, are the
work of architect No.6

131

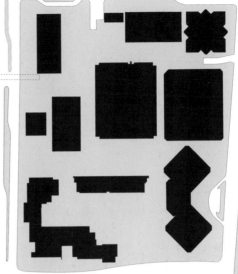
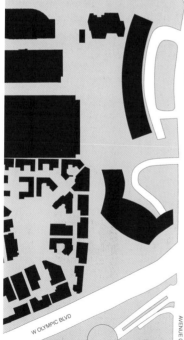
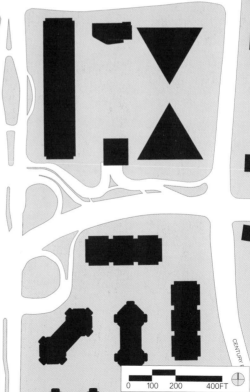

SANTA MONICA BLVD

CONSTELLATION BLVD

W OLYMPIC BLVD

AVENUE OF THE STARS

CENTURY

0   100   200   400FT

8a. Century City

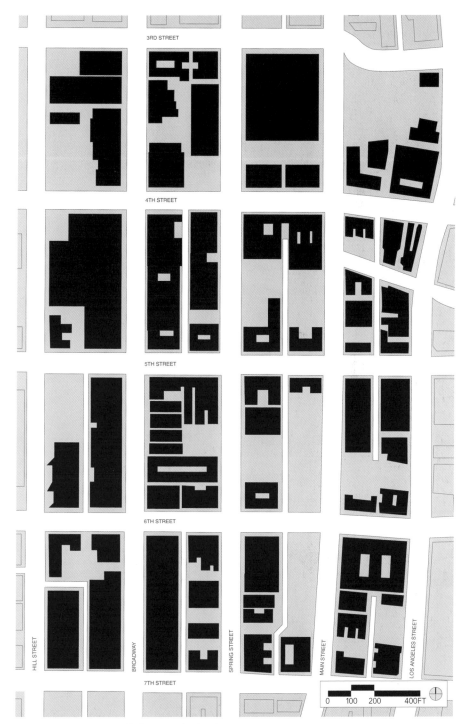

8b. Downtown Los Angeles

9a. Turtle Rock, Irvine

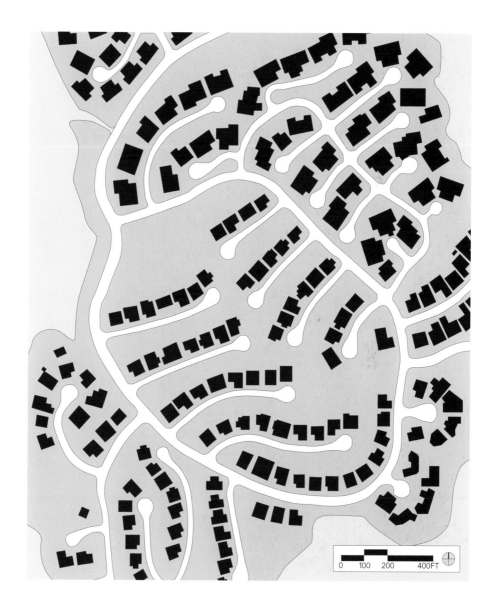

9b. Turtle Rock, Irvine (Enlargement)

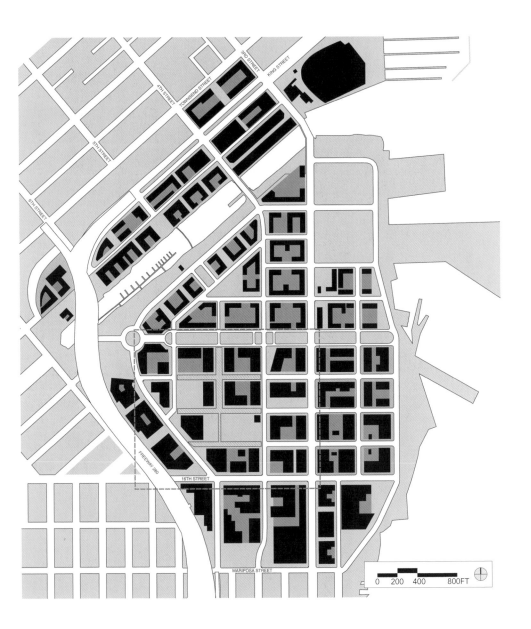

10. Mission Bay Master Plan, San Francisco

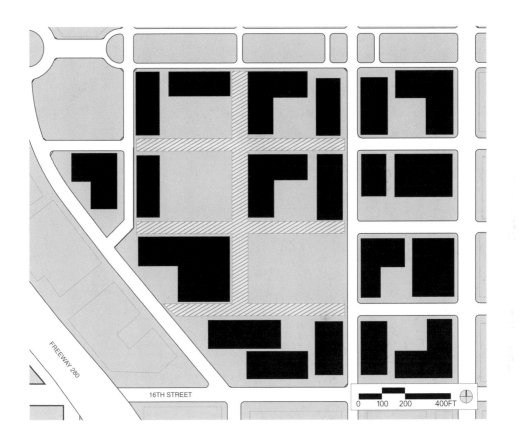

11. University of California, San Francisco, Mission Bay
Competition Winner, Machado Silvetti

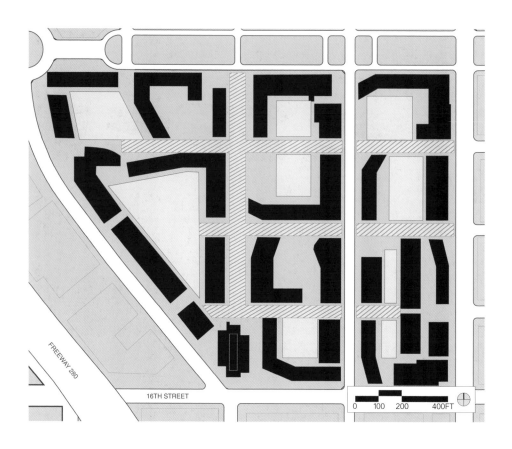

FREEWAY 280

16TH STREET

0   100   200   400FT

12. University of California, San Francisco, Mission Bay
Competition Entry, Steven Holl

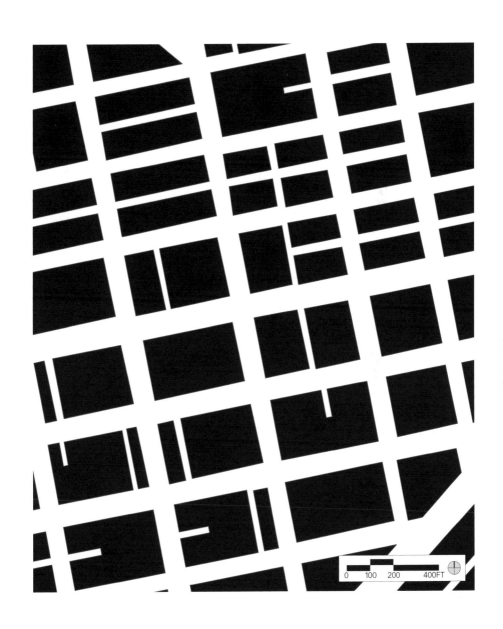

0 100 200 400FT

13. San Francisco Typical Block 275' x 412.5'

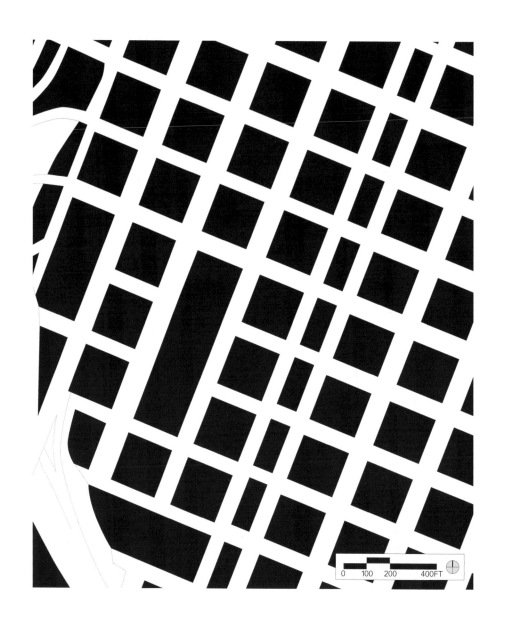

14. Portland Typical Block 200' x 200'

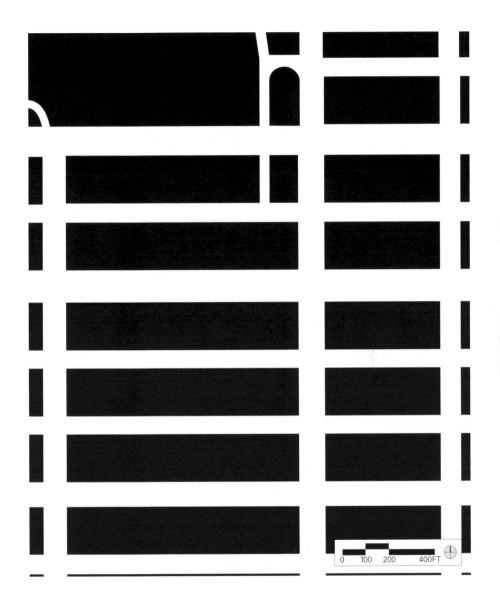

15. New York Typical Blocks 200' x 800' and 200' x 400'

16. Irvine Business Complex Typical Blocks 650' x 1200'

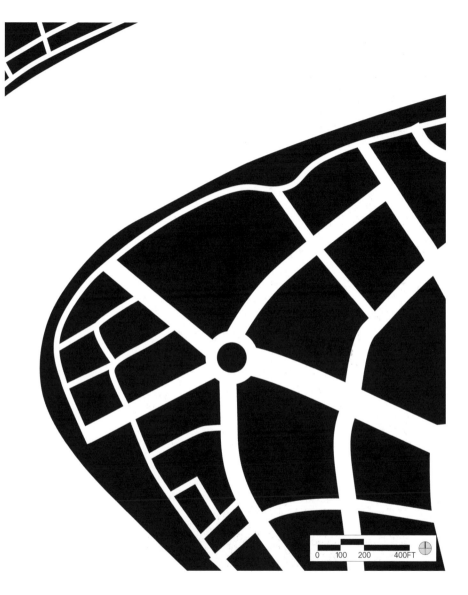

17. Pudong District, Shanghai

18. XinTianDi, PuXi, Shanghai

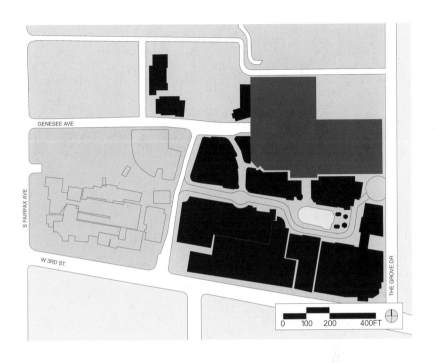

19. The Grove, Los Angeles

20. Universal CityWalk, Los Angeles

W BROADWAY

S CENTRAL AVE

S BRAND BLVD

COLORADO STREET

0   100   200   400FT

21. The Americana at Brand, Glendale

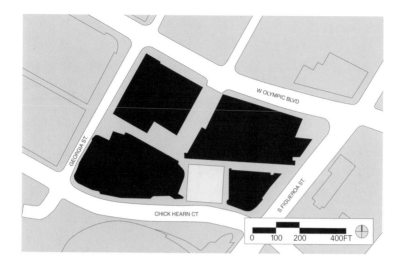

22. Nokia Plaza at L.A. Live

BIBLIOGRAPHY

Alexander, Christopher. "A City Is Not a Tree." *Architectural Forum 122.* April, 1965. No.1, 58-61 and No. 2, 58-62. Reprinted in *Design After Modernism.* Edited by John Thackara. London: Thames and Hudson, 1988.

A.T. Kearney, the Chicago Council on Foreign Affairs and *Foreign Policy. The Global Cities Index 2010. Foreign Policy*, August 2010. www.foreignpolicy.com/node/373401.

Associated Press. "Too much seasonal spirit: Abu Dhabi hotel 'regrets' £7m Christmas tree." *Guardian.co.uk*, Sunday 19 December 2010. www.guardian.co.uk/world/2010/dec/19/abu-dhabi-hotel-christmas-tree.

Barnett, Jonathan. *Urban Design as Public Policy: Practical Methods for Improving Cities.* New York: Architectural Record Books, 1974.

Belanger, Pierre. "Redefining Infrastructure." *Ecological Urbanism.* Baden, Switzerland: Lars Müller Publishers, 2010: 332-349.

Berger, Alan. *Drosscape: Wasting Land in Urban America.* New York: Princeton Architectural Press, 2007.

Bourriaud, Nicolas. *Relational Aesthetics.* Paris, France: Les Presses Du Reel, 1998. Retrieved online from the excerpt in www.creativityandcognition.com/blogs/legart/wp-content uploads/2006/07/Borriaud.pdf.

Brooks, David. *Bobos in Paradise: The New Upper Class and How They Got There.* New York: Simon & Schuster, 2000.

Carlson, Neil F. and **Don Terner**. *UHAB Comes of Age: Thirty Years of Self-Help Housing in New York.* New York, NY: UHAB, 2004. Retrieved online from www.community-wealth. org, a project of The Democracy Collaborative at the University of Maryland, College Park. www.community-wealth.org/ pdfs/articles-publications/coops/report-carlson.pdf.

Castells, Manuel. *The Rise of the Network Society.* Malden, MA: Blackwell Publishers, 1996.

Davey, Peter. "Berlin-Potsdamer Platz development."*Architectural Review*, January 1998. Retrieved online at www.findarticles.com/p/articles/mi_m3575/is_n1211_v203/ai_20390041/?tag=content;col1.

Drucker, Peter F. "Will the Corporation Survive?" *The Economist,* November 1, 2001. Made available online through The Drucker Institute. www.druckerinstitute.com/whydrucker/why_articles_corporationsurvive.html.

Durkeim, Emile. *The Elementary Forms of Religious Life.* Paris: F. Alcan, 1912. Karen E. Fields, Translation & Introduction. New York: The Free Press, 1995.

Fain, William H., Jr. *Tremont Street Special District.* Massachusetts: Boston Redevelopment Agency, 1976.

Friedman, Thomas L. "Teaching for America." *New York Times*, November 20, 2010. www.nytimes.com/2010/11/21/opinion/21friedman.html.

Fung, Brian and **Jared Mondschein**. "Metropolis Now: Images of the World's Top Global Cities." *Foreign Policy,*The Global Cities Index 2010, August 16, 2010. www.foreignpolicy.com/articles/2010/08/16/metropolis_now. ("7. Los Angeles")

German Federal Ministry of Transport, Building and Urban Affairs. "Shipyards to Sustainability: Bo01/Mälmo/Sweden." *"Baukulture" as an Impulse for Growth: Good Examples for European Cities.* April 2007: 14-15.

Giedion, Sigfried. *Space, Time and Architecture: The Growth of a New Tradition.* Fifth edition, revised and enlarged. Boston: Harvard University Press, 2002. First published 1941 by Harvard University Press.

Goldberger, Paul. "Eminent Dominion: Rethinking the legacy of Robert Moses." *The New Yorker*, February 5, 2007. www.newyorker.com/arts/critics/skyline/2007/02/05/070205crsk_skyline_goldberger.

Great Public Spaces Article "Rockefeller Center" in the Project for Public Spaces (PPS). Retreived online at www.pps.org/great_public_spaces/one?public_place_id=402.

Hawthorne, Christopher. "It has no place: Despite its name, L.A. Live is not of the city." *Los Angeles Times*, Architecture Review, December 03, 2008. www.articles.latimes.com/2008/dec/03/entertainment/et-lalive3.

Jacobs, Allan B. Great Streets. Cambridge, MA: MIT Press, 1995.

Jacobs, Jane. *The Death and Life of Great American Cities.* New York: Vintage Books, 1992. First published 1961 by Random House.

Jaime Lerner interviewed by Zara Bilgrami for CNN. "Maveric mayor: 'Eco-architecture not ego-architecture.'" June 6, 2008. www.cnn.com/2008/TECH/06/06/jaime.lerner/index.html.

Kane, Will. "Bay Area bridge tolls take a toll on commuters." *San Francisco Chronicle*, July 29, 2010: A-1.

Kayden, Jerold S., The Department of City Planning of the City of New York, The Municipal Art Society of New York. *Privately Owned Public Space: The New York City Experience.* New York: John Wiley & Sons, Inc., 2000.

Khanna, Parag. "Beyond City Limits: The age of nations is over. The new urban age has begun." *Foreign Policy*. September/October 2010. www.foreignpolicy.com/articles/2010/08/16/beyond_city_limits?page=full.

Knoflacher, Herman, Philip Rode and **Geetam Tiwari**. "How Roads Kill Cities." *The Endless City*. London: Phaidon Press, 2008: 340-347.

Koolhaas, Rem. *Delirious New York: A Retroactive Manifesto for Manhattan.* New York: Monacelli Press, 1994. First published 1978 by Academy Editions, London.

Koolhaas, Rem and Bruce Mau. *S,M,L,XL.* New York: Monacelli Press, 1998. 2nd Edition.

Kozinn, Allan. "Classical; Continental Shift."*New York Times*, Arts and Leisure Desk, January 15, 2006. www.nytimes.com/2006/01/15/arts/music/15kozi.html.

Koyen, Jeff. "Steal This Look: Will a wave of piracy lawsuits bring down Forever 21?" *Radar*, February 22, 2008. Retrieved online at www.sit-back-relax.tressugar.com/interesting-story-Forever-21-1074976.

Lao Tzu poem: "San-shih fu" or "Thirty Spokes." Translated by Raymond B. Blakney and published in *The Way of Life: Lao Tzu.* New York:Penguin Putnam (New American Library), 2001: 63.

Lee, Jennifer. *Civility in the City*: Blacks, Jews, and Koreans in Urban America. Cambridge, MA: Harvard University Press, 2002.

Leopold, Aldo. *Sand County Almanac*. New York: Ballantine Books, 1986. First published 1949 by Oxford University Press.

Logan, John R. and **Harvey L. Molotch**. *Urban Fortunes: The Political Economy of Place*. Los Angeles: University of California Press, 1987.

Los Angeles Economic Development Corporation. *Los Angeles County Profile*. www. laedc. org /reports/.

Malmuth, David and **Jack Skelley**. "The Capital of Creativity: Ethnic-focused development and residential innovation highlight southern California's economic dynamism." *Urban Land*, September 2005: 86-163.

MasterCard Worldwide. *2007 MasterCard Worldwide Centers of Commerce Index*. June 2007.

MasterCard Worldwide. *2008 MasterCard Worldwide Centers of Commerce Index*. June 2008.

Mayne, Thom. *Combinatory Urbanism*. Culver City: Stray Dog Café, 2011.

McWilliams, Carey. *Southern California: An Island on the Land*. Layton, UT: Gibbs Smith Publisher, 1973. First published 1946 by Duell, Sloan & Pearce, NY.

Mostafavi, Mohsen. "Why Ecological Urbanism? Why Now?" *Ecological Urbanism*. Baden, Switzerland: Lars Müller Publishers, 2010: 12-51.

O'Mara, Margaret. "Don't Try This at Home: You can't build a new Silicon Valley just anywhere." *Foreign Policy*, September/October 2010. www.foreignpolicy.com/articles/2010/08/16/dont_try_this_at_home?page=full.

Ouroussoff, Nicolai. "In Change Face of Beijing, a Look at the New China." *New York Times*, July 13, 2008. www.nytimes.com/2008/07/13/arts/design/13build.html?_r=1&ref=normanfoster.

Owens, Craig. "History of Century City."From the Century City Chamber of Commerce website, www.centurycitycc.com/wp-content/uploads/2010/10/HISTORY-OF-CENTURY-CITY.pdf.

Peñalosa, Enrique. "Politics, Power, Cities." *The Endless City*. London: Phaidon Press, 2008: 307-319.

Placemaker Profile Article "Enrique Peñalosa" in the Project for Public Spaces (PPS). Retrieved online at www.pps.org/articles/epenalosa-2/.

Representatives of the Iroquois Confederacy. "A Basic Call to Consciousness: The Hau de no sau nee Address to the Western World." Mohawk Nation: *Akwesasne Notes*, 1978, www.ratical.com/many_worlds/6Nations/BasicCtC.html.

Robbins, Richard H. *Global Problems and the Culture of Capitalism*. Boston: Allyn and Bacon, 1999. Quoted in Shah, Anup."Creating the Consumer."*Global Issues*, May 14, 2003. www.globalissues.org/article/236/creating-the-consumer.

Rockefeller Center website, "Art and History" selected pages, copyrighted by Tishman Speyer. www.rockefellercenter.com/art-and-history/.

Rousseau, Jean-Jacques. *The Social Contract, Or Principles of Political Right*. Translated by Maurice Cranston. New York: Penguin Classics, Modern Reprint Edition, 1968. First published 1762 in the Kingdom of France as *Du contrat social ouPrincipes du droitpolitique.*

Schor, Juliet. "The New Politics of Consumption: Why Americans want so much more than they need."*Boston Review*, Summer 1999. www.bostonreview.net/BR24.3/schor.html.

Schumacher, E.F. *Small is Beautiful: Economics as if People Mattered.* London: Blond & Briggs, 1973. Reprinted with introduction by Paul Hawken and commentaries. Point Roberts Washington: Hartley & Marks, 1999. Page references are to the 1999 edition.

Sennett, Richard. "Civility." *Urban Age*, Bulletin 1, Summer 2005: 1-3. Retrieved from the online publication archives of www.urban-age.nethttp://www.urban-age.net/0_downloads/archive/Richard_Sennett-Civility-Bulletin1.pdf.

Sennett, Richard. "The Open City." *The Endless City*. London: Phaidon Press, 2008: 290-297.

Soja, Edward W. "Designing the Postmetropolis." *Harvard Design Magazine*, Fall 2006/Winter 2007: 44-49.

Sorkin, Michael. "The End(s) of Urban Design." *Harvard Design Magazine*, Fall 2006/Winter 2007: 5-18.

Tilford, Dave. *Why Consumption Matters.* Dave Tilford, 2000. Available on the Sierra Club website. www.sierraclub.org/sustainable_consumption/tilford.asp.

Walsh, John (Editor), **Kira Perov** (Photographer) and **Peter Sellars** (Contributor). *Bill Viola: The Passions.* Los Angeles: Getty Publications, 2003.

Webber, Melvin M. "Planning in an Environment of Change, Part II: Permissive Planning." *Town Planning Review* 39(4) (1969): 277-295. Reprint made available by the Institute of Urban and Regional Development, University of California at Berkeley.

Wheatley, Allan. "China's golden age of consumption." *Reuters*, December 9, 2010. Retrieved online in the *Financial Post*. www.financialpost.com/China+golden+consumption/3952425/story.html.

Wikipedia contributors."Relational Art." *Wikipedia, The Free Encyclopedia*, www.en.wikipedia.org/wiki/Relational_Art (Accessed June 24, 2008).

COLLABORATORS AND CONTRIBUTORS

Although the ideas for these essays are drawn from my personal experience, there are many who have added to them as collaborators and critics, and I am indebted to all who have contributed.

An "Editorial Group" from my office was set up that included Trina Gunther and Mark Gershen. I involved both because of their inquisitive minds and ability to think broadly. Trina is a talented researcher with an exceptional ability to identify and develop a line of thinking. Mark challenged the content and word choice and excels at composition and word selection. I am grateful for their commitment to me in developing the manuscript. Merry Norris, a prominent Los Angeles art consultant, advised on art selection and was instrumental in obtaining the permissions of artists to reprint their works. My assistant, Akira Nakano, kept us on track and made sure all critical items were completed in the production process. Sarah Carr is a gifted U. K. graphic designer with great imagination, ability to visualize and patience with a rather opinionated client. From the outset she had a vision for this book that enhances and complements the material.

I am indebted to a number of prominent individuals whose own work was inspirational and who generously agreed to review the manuscript. Robert Campbell, architectural critic for the *Boston Globe*, has been aware of my career since he wrote an article about the Tremont Street Special District, a project done for the Boston Redevelopment Authority in the 1970s. He has a broad architectural perspective and understands the spatial and temporal qualities of cities. I am privileged that he agreed to write the Forward. Ray Kappe, an extraordinary designer and educator, stressed to me the impacts of unique political contexts on urban design assignments. I appreciate the work of Donlyn Lyndon for the environmental design of Sea Ranch, a precursor to the contemporary environmental movement, and his writings on urban "place-making."

Richard Koshalek offered his creative energy and references for art in the urban experience. I am indebted to historian Kevin Starr, who has eloquently articulated the importance of cultural memory in the design of cities. Thom Mayne, an extraordinary designer and teacher, provided observations drawing from his distinguished career in the pursuit of new urban form. Katherine Rinne contributed her knowledge and perspective on the evolution of cities. I am grateful to these individuals for the insights that adjusted and improved the manuscript.

I would like to acknowledge other professionals for their contributions: Martha Welborne for her insights into urban design and transportation planning; John Kaliski for his writings and conceptual thinking addressing the Los Angeles urban condition; Gunilla Kronvall for her work in sustainable urban design, particularly the waterfront development in Malmö, Sweden; Laurie Olin for his design of public spaces and commitment to a collaborative design process; And Rick Carter for an endless flow of ideas, and the discussions we have had about time, motion and place-making. Others who provided me mentoring over the years include Jaquelin T. Robertson, Richard Weinstein, Jonathan Barnett and Stephen Quick during the New York City Urban Design Group years; F.J. McCulloch from Central Lancashire, my staunch and principled professor at the University of Manchester; Steen Eiler Rasmussen, the Danish architect responsible for the Copenhagen "Fingers Plan"; Maurice Ash, Chairman of the Town and Country Planning Association in London; Weiming Lu, for his work in Richmond, Virginia and Dallas, Texas; and Don Terner, while he was a professor at MIT.

I am indebted to Scott Johnson, my partner at Johnson Fain, who encouraged and supported the writing of this book. In our practice of more than twenty years, many of the ideas from the essays were explored in the firm's projects. Hence there are and have been many collaborators in the practice.

Ann Gray heads Balcony Press, our publisher. She encouraged me to write several of the original essays in 2006 while she was publisher of *L.A. Architect* magazine. She has a keen understanding of the architectural media and provided valuable advice as the project progressed. Jennifer Caterino was the editor of those essays and was essential in copy editing this book. Peter Shamray managed the production process and steered us clear of numerous pitfalls.

Finally, I would like to acknowledge the contributions of my wife, Jennifer, and our two daughters, Elizabeth Fain LaBombard and Margaret Fain Jenkins. Elizabeth and Meg are both with design firms in New York City. Jennifer refers to herself as the "architect of our family" and is indeed the one who holds us all together. They also reviewed the manuscript drafts; their dedication, objectivity and encouragement helped me stay focused in bringing closure to this project.

INDEX